THE LIVING MIRROR

FIVE YOUNG POETS FROM LENINGRAD

THE LIVING MIRROR

Five Young Poets from Leningrad

SUZANNE MASSIE

Translations by Max Hayward
with Suzanne Massie and George L. Kline
Poetic versions by Paul Roche and John Statathos

DOUBLEDAY & COMPANY, INC.
GARDEN CITY, NEW YORK
1972

Bobby
Susanna
Elizabeth

Юле
Андрею
Евгению
Марине
Сергею

ACKNOWLEDGEMENTS

I WISH ESPECIALLY to express my gratitude to Max Hayward, Fellow of St Antony's College, Oxford. Not only did he translate many of the poems in this book, but it is in great part due to his invaluable help and advice from its earliest beginnings that this work has now been accomplished. I also wish to thank Professor Claude Frioux of the University of Vincennes and the Sorbonne for his guidance, and Professor George L. Kline of Bryn Mawr for his help in all that concerns the texts of Joseph Brodsky. I am also indebted to Madame Jean Etienne Don, and Laure Spindler, for their assistance with specific Russian texts. I am very grateful to Paul Roche, who, in addition to contributing numerous poetic versions, gave me his friendship and encouragement. My husband helped me greatly with editing and with many valuable comments and suggestions, and my children helped me too, by cheerfully understanding my dedication to this project. There were friends in many parts of the world who supported and helped me with their interest and enthusiasm. I thank them all.

S. M.

CONTENTS

NOTE

With the exception of the poems of Joseph Brodsky, all literal translations from the Russian were done by Suzanne Massie and Max Hayward. Paul Roche and John Statathos collaborated on some of the final poetic translations, and these translations are credited to them in the text. Poetic translations not otherwise credited are by Suzanne Massie.

All the translations of poems by Joseph Brodsky are the work of George L. Kline. His translations will be included in a forth-coming selection of Brodsky's poems to be published by Penguin Books in the Penguin Modern European Poets series.

THE LIVING MIRROR

FIVE YOUNG POETS FROM LENINGRAD

LENINGRAD

"The City makes the Soul."
Alexander Kushner

LENINGRAD IS A city—but it is also a state of mind. It is Russian, but it looks toward the West which is only a few miles away. It stands boldly facing the sea, in the north-western corner of a nation which stretches halfway across the world to the Pacific. Its very presence poses a defiant challenge to nature and man. Its architecture is grandiose, startling, beautiful; it is a city built of dreams made eternal in stone. A single man, the greatest Russian Tsar, Peter the Great, willed its creation but his vision became reality because of the hard work and sacrifice of many thousands of Russian people. Today, after suffering extraordinary devastation during our century, Leningrad is patiently being rebuilt and cared for. The city is not a monument to the Western architects who helped design it, but rather it is a monument to the imagination, ruthlessness, boldness and sense of beauty of the Russian people—of the sovereigns who ordered it, the artisans and workers who built it. It owes its continued existence today to that indomitable Russian spirit that has so often astonished and awed the world—a spirit which understands how to survive even the impossible ordeal.

It is a timeworn Western cliché to speak of Leningrad as "not Russian". Certainly it is not the pleasantly picturesque, the backward Russia of izbas and babushkas, of earthy proverbs spoken by peasants in bast shoes. It represents, instead, the loftiest spiritual and intellectual aspirations of the Russian soul . . . a thrust to the stars, a leap of centuries, a challenge to Europe.

Peter the Great consciously willed it so. It is a city built almost at a stroke—a young city, younger than New York. On May 16, 1703 Peter scratched a cross on the marshy land at the head of the Gulf of Finland, where the Neva River flows into the sea. He chose the site solely because of its proximity to the sea and to Europe. If he considered the difficulties of construction at all, it was only to dismiss them.

But the difficulties were extraordinary. The islands of the Neva channels are flat and the lowlying marshes are exposed to floods. The northerly location and the evaporation from the swamps make the climate damp and severe. Winter lasts from November to April. The Neva is frozen for six months. No matter, Peter was in a hurry. One hundred thousand, perhaps even two hundred thousand people lost their lives building the city on wooden piles sunk in the shifting, marshy ground—so many people, in fact, that it was said that the city was built on bones. And who counted the cost or kept statistics? Peter wanted his city immediately and so indeed, only twenty years after he scratched the cross in the marshes, there was a city. Peter wanted it to rival the most beautiful cities in the West and he imported the finest architects he could find. Under dire threats, he ordered his nobles to leave Moscow, and build houses of stone in St Petersburg.

From the first it was to be a city of ideas. Peter created the first learned Academies in Russia, the first libraries. He staffed his educational institutions with foreign teachers and intended Petersburg's contact with all that was good in the West to be close and fruitful. From the moment of its founding and throughout its history this city has been the focus of the struggle between the conservative heritage of Russia and the liberal ideas fostered by the Enlightenment in Europe.

After Peter's death in 1725, the construction continued unceasingly. In the years 1741–61 the swamps were drained and the streets paved. The Admiralty, with its lofty shimmering golden spire became the landmark of the centre, with wide avenues radiating from it. These three main avenues, the Nevsky, Mayorov and Dzerzhinsky, along with three great canals, the Moika, Griboyedov and Fontanka, remained the nucleus, with other streets and canals added. Baroque, and later classical buildings were erected, giving the city a strong regular appearance reminiscent of ancient Palmyra. The famous embankments of grey and pink Finnish marble were built along the Neva. Building spread over the numerous islands—Apothecaries, Petrograd, Vassilevsky, Kameny, Elagin—which were all then connected by stone and wooden floating bridges. (Today there are 480 bridges.)

As it grew, the city's wide straight avenues combined severe and stately buildings and planned squares with green parks adorned with white marble statues and sparkling fountains. In the countryside, surrounding the city like a necklace of rare jewels, a group of summer palaces were created: Peterhof, Tsarskoe Selo, Gatchina, Oranienbaum, Pavlovsk.

Yet for a city to achieve greatness, there must be more than architecture. Petersburg–Petrograd–Leningrad has always been far more than a mere collection of stone buildings and monuments. About it is an atmosphere that excites and continually creates new dreams. There is the marriage of sky and water: pure sky filled with swiftly-moving, changing clouds—and water, moving in summer, hibernating in winter, but always alive under the ice. Water and sky reflect each other and a human being is forever suspended between them. There is the sobriety of the unadorned streets with their rows of stern buildings whose rich façades then surprise and delight the eye with their profusion of colour—façades of yellow and white, bright green and blue, lavender and dark red. There is the mellow, golden warmth of the city in summer when it is full of lupin and poppies, lilacs and wild roses, whose scent, blown by the fresh wind of the Neva, fills the city and perfumes the White Nights of perpetual dawn. Every monument, every street speaks of the past, of poetry, of music, of adventure. In it, one feels the seductive pull of the impossible. If a city like this can exist where no city should have existed, what can man not do?

The inhabitants of such a city cannot easily be separated from it. They are what they are, they think what they think, because these sights are not only in their eyes, but in their souls. They sing of the city, write about it, love it.

Pushkin wrote:

> The Neva is clad in granite,
> Bridges hang poised over her waters,
> Her islands are covered with dark green gardens,

And before the younger capital, ancient Moscow
Has paled, like a purple clad widow
Before a new Empress.

I love you city of Peter's creation. I love your stern harmonious
aspect.
. . . the transparent twilight and moonless gleam of your pensive
nights.

The Bronze Horseman

For 200 years (1718–1918), St Petersburg was the capital of
Russia, and the centre of all that was best culturally, artistically,
and scientifically. A contemporary poet of Leningrad once said,
"Know this city. Here you will walk the footsteps of the great
and by knowing it, you will know Russia." Here were born or
worked most of Russia's greatest talents of the eighteenth, nineteenth and early twentieth centuries: Pushkin, Lermontov,
Nekrasov, Tolstoy, Gogol, Dostoevsky, Tchaikovsky, Borodine,
Rimsky-Korsakov, Moussorgsky, Glinka, Stravinsky, Prokofiev,
Shostakovitch, Nijinsky, Pavlova, Karsavina, Diaghilev, Mayakovsky, Blok, Yesenin, Akhmatova, Mandelstam, Repin, Serov,
Bakst, Goncharov, Pavlov and Mendeleyev. Is it possible to call
their city "not Russian"? The revolution was born in Petersburg
because nowhere else in Russia did political and philosophical ideas
flourish as in Petersburg's atmosphere.

If Petersburg is not Russian, is Moscow? An historian could
convincingly argue that Moscow is not as Russian as ancient Kiev,
a modern economist that Moscow is not as Russian as modern
Novosibirsk. Kiev was the beloved eldest child, a golden dream
forever killed by the Mongols; Moscow was the middle child of
the thirteenth century, jealous and never quite secure. Russia's
graceful offspring of the eighteenth century was Petersburg.

★   ★   ★

> . . . and put under a spell by Empress Eudoxia,★
> Dostoyevskian and possessed,
> The city retreated into its mists.
> *"Poem Without a Hero", Anna Akhmatova*

Like Sleeping Beauty, Petersburg was showered with gifts at birth, but it seems that there was also a jealous evil fairy to lay a curse on it. From the beginning it has had a heavy share of tragedy for so young a city. Nature has attacked it. It is a prey to recurrent floods (the floods of 1824 and 1924 were particularly severe) which periodically have swept away whole neighbourhoods. Even today, flood marks are painted on the sides of buildings. Twice its name has been changed. First, in 1914, when Nicholas II in a burst of patriotic feeling decreed that the name should be changed from the German Petersburg to the Russian Petrograd. Then again in 1924, at the time of Lenin's death, when it was changed to Leningrad. "We wanted to honour him," explained a Soviet official, "so we gave him the best we had."

But even before Lenin's death, a change in the city's status had begun. It was a tragedy for Petrograd—one still deeply felt by its citizens—that in March 1918, Lenin decided to "temporarily" move the capital back to Moscow. In Moscow, the revolution began to take on a different cast. For, if from the moment of its founding Petersburg was to be a special city with special people, it was also to become for Moscow the enduring symbol of all that was new, stylish and dangerous. Moscow had never learned to trust the glamorous northern city which for so long had supplanted it. Yet it was not until Stalin came to power that the suppressed rivalry became deadly.

Stalin feared Leningrad as a potential rival power base and took steps to downgrade it to the level of a provincial city. When the capital was officially transferred to Moscow, whole libraries went too. During the 1930's, cultural establishments were gradually

★ Peter the Great's first wife, a product of the old Muscovite culture, whom Peter divorced and later sent to a convent before embarking on his Westernizing policies, the most dramatic of which was the building of St Petersburg. Not surprisingly, Eudoxia always hated the new city.

transferred. Petersburg, the traditional home of the Russian ballet, had to accept that from then on, the younger Bolshoi was officially to supplant the proud, historic Imperial Ballet. When Moscow became the place where appropriations were decided, money for Leningrad became less available and then not available at all, thus effectively choking off artistic and cultural activities.

Cultural downgrading was only a prelude to political suppression. Leningrad was to become the first victim in Kremlin struggles as bloody as any in the time of Ivan the Terrible.

The terrible purges of the thirties began in Leningrad with the mysterious assassination in 1934 of Sergei Kirov, Leningrad Party Secretary. At first it was party members, but swiftly the arrests began to concentrate heavily on young people, intellectuals —anyone who had shown lack of sympathy with the régime. These purges swept over Russia like a terrible plague. It is estimated that before Stalin had finished more than 13,000,000 people had disappeared—the best of an entire generation.

Yet even Stalin's 1937 Terror was not to be the end of Leningrad's political ordeal. Keeping an implacably hostile watch on the city, Stalin picked Andrei Zhdanov, one of his sternest lieutenants, as party boss for Leningrad. Zhdanov remained through most of the war years.

After the war, there remained in Leningrad a wartime exhilaration born of shared struggles, and a hope that the cultural easing which had begun under cover of the superior outside threat would continue. From 1943 onwards, the great Leningrad poet Anna Akhmatova, the satirist Mikhail Zoschenko, as well as Moscow's Boris Pasternak, had been quietly published in the magazines *Zvezda* and *Leningrad*. But in 1946 Zhdanov's hand was again to fall on Leningrad, in a period of extreme pressure and of intimidation in art and culture known today as the *zhdanovschina*. Zhdanov described Akhmatova as "half nun, half whore". The magazine *Leningrad* was completely liquidated and the editor of *Zvezda* was replaced by a tough, uncompromising hardliner. Akhmatova and Zoschenko were expelled from the Writers' Union.

Even this was not to be enough. In Moscow, while Stalin

looked on, Zhdanov and Georgi Malenkov engaged in a deadly struggle for power. In August 1948 Zhdanov's death was announced. Malenkov took over Leningrad and there followed yet another period of extreme humiliation and arrests. The severity of this new period of purges may be measured by the fact that Akhmatova herself was forced in 1951-2 to write poems in praise of Stalin. This she did, but in a style so unlike her own that it was clear they had been written under pressure. Her only son was arrested. She was left at liberty, but her livelihood was taken away and she had to survive on the charity of her friends.

This period, though far less known and publicized than the first, was perhaps the most ruthless of all the Leningrad purges. It is known today as the "Leningrad Affair". If the details of the internecine struggles for power that caused it are still veiled in secrecy, the results are not. The entire party apparatus of Leningrad was totally destroyed—all were arrested or executed. The morale of the Leningrad party was broken completely.

Until he was appointed Soviet ambassador to Peking in September 1970, Leningrad was tightly controlled by a conservative leader named Vassily Tolstikov. A stern man who was known popularly as "the master", he is reputed once to have growled, "Leningrad is the cradle of the revolution—and no one will be allowed to rock the cradle."

*   *   *

For Leningrad, the greatest disaster of this—or perhaps any—century was the German Siege of 1941-3. But from this nightmare emerged a common glory which turned disaster into triumph. For 900 grim and heroic days the city lived isolated, besieged, starving, dying. Miraculously, it survived. It was a time when people by the thousands froze to death in the streets and in their homes. For months, the bread ration dropped to a single piece of bread per person. Starving children ate sugar-saturated dirt around the destroyed sugar warehouses. All the cats and dogs and pigeons were eaten, and Leningrad children grew up without knowing what they looked like. Even today there are very few.

During the Siege, Leningrad became one family. Harrison Salisbury, in *The 900 Days*, quotes a student who wrote, "All of us Leningraders are one family, baptized by the monstrous blockade—one family, one in our grief, one in our experience, one in our hope and expectations." He adds that some even suggested that Leningrad boys should henceforth marry nothing but Leningrad girls—so much had they become a special breed.

When it was over, they were confronted with acres of ruins, and a staggering toll of disaster. The Germans had destroyed the housing of 716,000 people, 526 schools, 101 museums. Gone were the Pulkovo Astronomical Observatory, the Botanical and Zoological Institutes, and much of Leningrad University. Of 300 eighteenth- and nineteenth-century buildings classified as historical monuments, 187 had vanished along with 849 factories and 71 bridges. But far more terrible was the human toll—after the siege, three out of four people in Leningrad were dead. The population in 1944 had gone down to an estimated 560,000 people—down from two million before the war.

Among those who survived those terrible days was forged an unbreakable civic pride. Eighteenth-century Petersburg was built by the sacrifice of thousands of lives—its beauty was their monument. Two centuries later the people of Leningrad paid again with hundreds of thousands of lives to prevent this beauty from being violated and conquered by the Germans. Modern Leningrad is today a monument to this achievement—and no one in the city forgets this fact. Even today, as a reminder, there are signs on the "sunny" side of the Nevsky and Sadovaya Prospects. In neat blue and white lettering, carefully repainted, they warn, "Citizens: In case of shelling, this side of the street is the most dangerous."

At first it was proposed that palaces be left in ruins as monuments to German brutality, but it is a victory for hope and beauty that this plan was rejected. From the first days after the war the people of Leningrad set to work to rebuild the monuments and the city they love so tenaciously. Hampered often by lack of funds, the work has been slow. This task of artistic reconstruction is perhaps the most ambitious and touching work of reconstruction ever attempted. Workers have been trained especially in the skills of the eighteenth century, materials have been found, old arts completely relearned. The plans for the restoration of certain palaces go beyond the year 2000. Although the need for housing remains urgent (the population of Leningrad is now limited by law, and as in other major Soviet cities a special permit is required to live there), architects have been mindful of their responsibilities. Buildings in the city proper were limited in height according to the width of the street. The great blocks of new housing developments have gone up on the outskirts of the city, creating whole new suburbs and living areas which do not mar the architectural unity of the older historic section.

The poet Olga Berggolts, who lived through the siege, on seeing the total destruction of the palaces of Peterhof and Tsarskoe Selo (now renamed Pushkin) wrote:

> Again from the black dust, from the place
> Of death and ashes will arise the garden as before.
> So it will be. I firmly believe in miracles
> You gave me that belief, my Leningrad.

The physical reconstruction of the city is not the only miracle. The series of disasters—purges, war, destruction, and again the purges that followed—very nearly severed all the artistic links with the past. The period of constant literary ferment and creativity in Moscow and Leningrad of the twenties along with the ideas of the Acmeists and the Futurists, were almost buried forever. Artists of all kinds left for lonely exile abroad. Mayakovsky committed suicide in Moscow, Yesenin in Leningrad. Tsvetayeva returned from Paris only to live in poverty and despair in Elabuga where she too committed suicide. Mandelstam died in a concentration camp near Vladivostok. The books of Khlebnikov, Biely, Kruchenykh, Zabolotsky were destroyed.

But there were a few who were spared. For Leningrad, the most important was Anna Akhmatova, who continued to live in her beloved city until her death in 1966. These precious few provided in themselves living links to the past. Akhmatova wrote, in her great poem *Requiem*:

No, I lived not under foreign skies,
Sheltering under foreign wings
I then stayed with my people
There where my people, unhappily, were.

She shared the trials, survived, and most important, continued to write until her death. She and a few indomitable others preserved the ideas and passed on some of the élan of the Silver Age—that productive period which began about 1890 and lasted into the 1920's—along with a knowledge and love of a Russian literary language which was very nearly destroyed during Stalin's purges. The artistic importance to Leningrad of Akhmatova's courageous decision becomes clearer every day.

For despite everything, Leningrad has remained an intellectual city, the home of some of the most important learned institutes in the Soviet Union. A Leningrad writer lives in an atmosphere of universities and schools. Many of the learned societies of the Soviet Union have their headquarters in Leningrad. There are thirteen theatres and forty-eight museums. The Saltykov-Shchedrin Library, founded in 1795, has twelve million volumes and many rare manuscripts.

It is still a city of great teachers, with a traditional interest in foreign languages and literature. There is a long and fine history of translation—among the many English translations in progress are the works of Poe, Frost, Milne, Byron, Milton, Donne and Allen Ginsberg—as well as work from Italian, French and German, the Slavic tongues, Georgian, Armenian and other languages of the Soviet republics. A number of contemporary poets, among them Brodsky, Kuzminsky and Betaki began and still support themselves primarily by working on translations. It is natural that, under these circumstances, Leningrad writers are particularly attentive to the quality of their own language and sensitive to any erosion of their literary past.

The five poets in this book are artistic representatives of a transition generation in Leningrad. All but one still in their thirties, they are war babies, born in the period from 1936 to the early 1940's.

The nightmare of the Blockade dominated their childhoods. Their generation is a generation which lost parents and family to the war, survived starvation and illness, had its schooling disrupted and has seen all the values of their elders—both pre-revolutionary and revolutionary—destroyed or dismantled. They have grown to maturity in a turbulent post-war period of re-evaluation and reconstruction.

During these post-war years, intelligent Russian youth has increasingly been searching for roots. They have looked to the ancient history of Russia, manifesting profound, although perhaps agnostic, interest in icons and old Russian architecture. Made rootless by purges, war and death, by easy marriage and easy divorce, they have had a mounting desire for meaningful ceremonies. They are searching to determine the eternal values in life—and in art, particularly Russian art.

This thoughtful generation is old enough to have felt and understood as children the atmosphere of the past, but young enough to have escaped the mortifying, numbing effects of the intellectual terrors imposed on their parents. Their eyes are opened; they are not easily fooled. The police no longer terrify in the total way of Stalin's time; they are simply there, inescapable, a familiar part of everyday life. They oppress, they swoop implacably, but life has managed to continue nevertheless.

In Leningrad, and in Russia, as in every country in the Western world, there is a marked gap which yawns between this generation and their elders. Russia, like the United States, is now a nation in which half the population is under twenty-six. In Russia this young population is entirely ruled by a generation mainly in their sixties with whom no dialogue is possible. Often repeated, the slogans of the Revolution have lost their glitter. Often betrayed, the Revolution has become the "establishment".

All five of the poets presented in this book have shared all the common experiences of their generation. They have been soldiers, worked in factories, in the snow and mud as ordinary labourers. Some have worked as geologists and made expeditions to the Arctic, Central Asia and to the Pacific borders of the Soviet Union. One studied biology and worked as a hydrologist in the Black Sea. It would be too easy and not quite accurate to call them "worker poets" but neither are they what is called "intellectual" in the Western sense. Only one of these poets has had a complete formal university education. Two have studied for a time at scientific institutes, one was trained as a furniture worker, another as a metal worker. Their varied experiences and intimate knowledge of the life of the ordinary working man gives to their work a freshness, originality and vigour quite often absent from contemporary Western literature.

There are many poets of all ages writing in Leningrad today, but the five poets in this book were chosen because they represent a variety of poetic methods and points of view. They all are exerting an influence on the thinking of the younger poets of Leningrad today. The most striking feature about them is how different they are from one another; also that although they acknowledge a number of literary influences, these influences are far less apparent than is the influence of Mayakovsky and Pasternak on Yevtushenko and Voznesensky. They are alike in their consciousness that they are the heirs of Petersburg. Otherwise they are completely individual in their approach to their art.

Victor Sosnora is a modern, complex, twentieth-century urban poet seeking the roots of contemporary society and the place of man in it. Often surreal, his work is full of symbols.

Gleb Gorbovsky, like Yesenin, is a Russian country lad who seems caught in the city. He has a very Russian feeling for nature, melancholy, biting with a peasant's shrewd and sometimes suspicious feelings about the threatening world.

Alexander Kushner admires and strives for the "clarism" effects of the Acmeists. A gentle, scholarly poet, he uses plain classical language with no symbolism, no misty allusions.

Joseph Brodsky, a protégé of Akhmatova, combines the elegance of image, simplicity and flow of line that is the best of the Petersburg tradition. He also reflects the traditional Petersburg interest in Western culture and is profoundly interested in and influenced by the English Metaphysical Poets.

Constantine Kuzminsky, a lyric poet and esthete, is preoccupied with the sound and form of language. He is seeking a new literary language and is influenced by the thinking and the language experiments. of the Russian Futurists. He admires the "sweet sounds" of Swinburne, Byron and Houseman.

They are not close friends, but they know each other. They attend each other's readings, listen to and read each other's work, occasionally exchange advice and opinions—but never agree about methods. One thing they all share is an overwhelming interest in their own country. Perhaps it would be more precise to say their heritage. They have reopened the old question: what is Russia? With the exception perhaps of Brodsky, they are not much influenced by or interested in foreign works. This is not only because they are denied free contacts, but more importantly because their greatest concern is to explore their own national personality. To use an historical phrase, this is a Slavophile rather than a Westernizer period. These poets are interested in every aspect of their country's artistic history and refuse to be denied it. They refuse to negate any of the achievements of the Russian past, whether in architecture, painting, music or poetry, and they are trying to evaluate these achievements in the light of their own concept of the twentieth century.

Products of Soviet society, they have never, as their predecessors Mayakovsky, Yesenin and Akhmatova, been allowed to travel abroad. Only one of them, Sosnora, has ever seen a western country. Yet they have travelled widely in their own immense nation and are at home in its roughest terrain.

Their works spring first from a passionate love of country, of the Russian language, character and people, of the grandeur and melancholy of the Russian landscape. None of this artistic experimentation and thinking can be called "anti-Soviet" unless being anti-Soviet means being pro-Russian.

They are all seeking links with the past, trying to pick up the severed threads of the poetic discussions of the twenties and thirties and to weave them into the discussions of the future. They are preoccupied with language, style and culture on which they place enormous importance. This word, culture, recurs over and over in conversation: "He has no culture" or "He has much culture", this or that professor "gives us culture".

All of these poets refer to themselves as "very old" in comparison with the new "young" poets (those in their twenties). Kuzminsky says simply, "They will accomplish more than I." Yet they themselves are the most important and indeed now the only links between what survived of the old and what promises to be the very new. With one hand they are reaching over the yawning chasm of catastrophes for their precursors while stretching with the other hand to those who will follow them. "What can we do?" asked one, "our fathers they killed, and our teachers, so we must be pupils and teachers at once."

Some have given readings frequently because they are gifted readers as well as poets; others by nature are more retiring and have read little in public. Three are already members of the Writers' Union; two are not yet. Some have been widely published, others less, but all are widely known among the youth of the city who accord them something of the renown, idolatry and affection accorded to popular singers in the West.

These poets are often closely allied in interests with the new generation of young engineers, scientists, and technicians who are their most loyal followers. With such devoted audiences they often feel a sense of mission, a necessity to teach. One of the poets explained, "I like audiences against whom I must struggle. Young engineers and technicians—they know everything but they know nothing. They are the best audiences. You can excuse the peasants and simple people for not knowing, but not those who have an education. I must throw at their heads things difficult to understand."

A poet can speak as selectively as this because of the massive popular interest in poetry which exists in Russia. It is a sort of national hobby. Poetry is a vital, living subject of discussion—people take strong sides, have violent differences of opinion on the merits of one poet or another. One of the most difficult things for a Westerner to explain to young Russians is our lack of this sort of day to day interest in poetry. They simply cannot understand why it is not a vital subject of conversation for us.

26

Perhaps the answer lies at least in part in Solzhenitsyn's belief that poetry is born of the torment of the soul. Poetry is meant to communicate a state of feeling or mind too strong or subtle to be expressed in prose. The Russian experience, the Russian land with its limitless horizons, intense winter and brief summer inspires incomparably strong emotions which the Russian has learned to distill into music and poetry. The language, strongly stressed, sonorous and flexible, lends itself admirably.

Poetry is a familiar part of everyday life not only of an elite group, but of a wide part of the population. Almost daily, along with the news, the radio in Leningrad broadcasts poetry. Obviously this poetry is of an official sort; the aesthetic level is not always very high. But the broadcast itself is an indication of poetry's importance. "Russians live on poetry," said one young Leningrad writer. It is rare to meet a Russian with any education whatsoever who cannot quote extensively from one poet or another. There are some who argue that this fact in itself means little; that it is the worst poets who are the most popular, that the public which rushes to listen to poets cannot distinguish the good from the bad. Nevertheless, they *do* rush to listen to poets of every kind. For a Russian, poetry is a familiar friend; it is useless to argue that the friend is sometimes vulgar.

A feature of the Soviet system is that every person is required, along with his work in a factory, office or university, to have cultural outlets and activities. In all factories and offices, as well as in schools, poetry is offered as one of these activities. In Leningrad, first in popularity after sports is poetry—ahead of music, painting or dancing. It seems incredible, but in the city today there are over 6,000 people at work writing poetry more or less regularly. Obviously, the number itself indicates that much of this poetry is amateurish, but the enthusiasm creates an enormous audience for poets of real talent. The popularity of poets is such that their books are always sold out within a day or two of printing—even when the editions are 50,000 or more. Anything below that figure is considered "very small". Someone explained to me very seriously once that it was impossible to get the book of such and such a poet because the printing was only a "tiny" ten thousand copies.

The many amateur poetry circles meet regularly to listen to each other's verses, to criticize and to learn. From these groups over the past ten years have emerged perhaps 3,000 poets who have been judged good enough to be printed at one time or another in the trade journals of their factories or even sometimes in the literary journals of Leningrad. The most important of these journals are the monthlies: *Zvezda* (Star) and *Neva*, both extremely conservative; the annual magazine *Den Poezii* (Day of Poetry), which prints a wider selection of poetry; the almanac *Molodoy Leningrad* (Young Leningrad).

These poetry groups number from as few as twenty members to as many as one hundred with an average group numbering fifty or sixty. Today there are one hundred such groups working in Leningrad. Members of the Writers' Union serve as group leaders and they receive an extra thirty-five to seventy roubles a month for performing this service. Group leaders meet once or twice a month with their circles in factory culture clubs and libraries. Most of these groups are completely unprofessional, everyone interested is welcome to come and read, ability being no criterion. Yet the character and degree of interest of the group leader can be a decisive factor in the development and literary success of his group. An interested group leader can be influential in having poets from his own group published, and in supporting them for membership in the Union itself. Group leaders can, in fact, seek out the most talented writers for a given circle. Within the past ten years several of these more sophisticated groups have developed—ones in which membership is tantamount to being published. In these select groups, the attitude is not merely "come and read" before being accepted, but "can you write and what is your talent?" In recent years, one such influential group leader has been Gleb Semeonov, in his early fifties and a poet himself. He has been known to interview one hundred fledglings and accept only twenty-five. His groups in the past have included Gorbovsky (1955–8), Sosnora (1959) and Kushner. Being accepted into the Semeonov group was an important step up the literary ladder. In 1969–70, Semeonov was concentrating on a group in their early twenties who had never been printed. Some other group leaders have followed this pattern and have also begun a sort of informal auditioning.

After Khrushchev's thaw, in 1959, public readings sponsored by various organizations became more frequent. Many poets who were not yet printed were invited along with official poets to come and read their verses and translations of foreign works. These readings helped them become known, and to make contacts with people in the literary world. It is a prevalent practice to tape these evenings, with the results that the poets themselves often have no idea how or which of their works have been copied and are circulating.

Although readings are popular in Leningrad, there is none of the massive excitement of the famous Moscow readings of Yevtushenko and Voznesensky. The audiences are smaller—four hundred people is an extremely large reading. These readings take place not in auditoriums, but in factory clubs, in theatres, in libraries. Poetry is recited quietly, not declaimed. Often it is simply read. This, too, is a Petersburg tradition. Akhmatova pronounced herself against flamboyance. This quiet poetry is being read to a new generation by a new generation of poets. Akhmatova once said, "You have seen the Silver Age—they will be the Golden Age."

Perhaps her proud prediction will yet prove to be true, but to be considered officially a poet, it is necessary to be accepted into the Writer's Union, which in Leningrad now has four hundred members. A poet is usually accepted after he has had two books published, but—and this can be a very big condition—his work must first be accepted by a Board of Editors, all of whom are already in the Writers' Union. Being accepted into the Union is primarily a social step forward, a useful mark of acceptance. A writer then can benefit from certain practical advantages of membership: he may borrow up to 1,000 roubles repayable from future earnings; an apartment may be made available to him, or he may be helped financially to acquire one; he may be given the use of a dacha in the summer colony at Komarovo on the Gulf of Finland. But he still must make his living from his published works, payment for which is determined on a single scale, no matter whether the writer is known or unknown. Original poetry is paid at the rate of 1 ruble, 40 kopecks* a line, translation of poetry at the rate of from 70 kopecks to 1 ruble 40 a line. Prose is paid at the rate of 300 rubles for 25 pages. A writer also can make additional money by writing criticism, reviews, and poems for newspapers and literary magazines.

Still, among the most influential figures in the Leningrad Writers' Union are a group of men in their late fifties and sixties. Some of these men fought on the front. Their love for their city is intense, but with a few exceptions they are extremely conservative, and mistrust change. Their artistic views are conditioned by the doctrine of socialist realism. In his speech at the First Congress of Soviet Writers in May 1934, Zhdanov curtly defined this doctrine:

"Socialist realism demands of the artist a truthful and historically concrete representation of reality in its revolutionary development. In addition, it must aid the process of ideological transformation and the education of the workers in the spirit of socialism."

To illustrate some of the themes of socialist realism it is perhaps useful to give a few examples of poems written by some of the influential members of the Leningrad Writers' Union, printed in the annuals *Den Poezii* and *Molodoy Leningrad*. One of the most important features of socialist realism is exhortation and congratulation to the Communist party for its accomplishments, as in this poem by the late Alexander Prokofiev, who from 1954 until 1964 was head of the Leningrad Writers' Union. This poem, entitled *To the Komsomol* appeared on the title page of *Molodoy Leningrad*, 1968:

> I love the straightness of thy path
> My Komsomol,
> Comrade mine.

* The U.S.S.R. has arbitrarily established the official value of one ruble (100 kopecks) at $1.18.

. . . .
Multi-millioned Komsomol
In the dread storm
You led tanks
across the Dnieper, Dniester,
and Don,
. . . .
You gave an example of courage
'Gainst Tigers and Panthers
'Gainst the mad destruction
You, Komsomol, were valorous!

Very important in socialist realism is civic pride of a "God Bless America" variety. Again, a selection from a poem by Alexander Prokofiev which appeared in *Den Poezii*, 1968:

I rank as a Leningrader
I have been counted by you.
Leningrad, I live
under your protection.

May your blue skies
Be blue, so blue,
May your woods be greener
With each year.

May your sun, dispensing joy,
Rise higher.

The all-important theme of optimism is remarkably well illustrated in the following fragments of a poem by Nikolai Braun, which appeared in *Den Poezii*, 1968. Braun is a senior member of the Writers' Union, and an omnipresent member of the editorial boards of the literary journals. The title of the poem is *I Love to Return Presents*:

I love to return presents,
You give me a spark

I give you a bonfire
If I'm given a pinch of something
I hand back a fistful
. . . .
If a friend is true in friendship
I do not believe in evil tongues,
If a hand is stretched out to me
I stretch out two.

In the poems of these socialist realist writers, particularly in those of the men who experienced the war, one senses a nostalgia for the good old days when values were clear and men were men —before the younger generation went to the dogs. This spirit is not at all unlike that of the so-called "silent majority" in the United States who also wistfully recall the days when supposedly there were no confusing or conflicting values in society. In this poem by Vadim Sheffner, who continually appears on editorial boards, there is the jocular, folksy tone and the nostalgia of the old fighting man:

The Pensioner
The infantry barber
Likes his little nip
and doesn't much like
to remember the war
He has a right to be proud
And has earned his rest
. . . .
Oh, the hair he cut,
He worked like a machine
No fancy cuts, mind you
But all crew cuts.

Oh, Infantry, Infantry!
Construction material!
In the hills and bogs,
He lost his clients.

These fancy haircuts
Are not for those kids—
Under the earth in their tunics
These twenty years they have been asleep.

Now it sort of makes me sad
Pour me out another one
Oh Infantry, oh Infantry
Queen of the fields!

Within the socialist realist school in Leningrad, there are two sub-divisions. One is the so-called "Peasant Poetry"—with its strong socialist themes, the themes of simple people hard at work amid the joys of nature. This was the only poetry printed during the late 1930's and early 1940's. Then came the war, and with it, a school of "War Poetry". This was work written by good soldiers, most of them with little general culture. They wrote patriotic, exhorting poems and poems describing their war experiences. Among these were Dleglin, Dudin, Tarasov and Sergei Orlov, a modest, retiring war poet who is still regularly printed today, although most of his poems date from the mid-forties. These war poets were and are still very influential in the Leningrad Writers' Union. For years "Peasant Poetry" and "War Poetry" were the only poetry in Leningrad and even today these two schools heavily dominate the thinking at the Union and the teaching in the groups.

As for lyric poetry, from 1946 and 1956, there was no lyric poetry at all. Indeed, at the time of Akhmatova's denunciation in 1947 a member of the Leningrad Writers' Union declared unconditionally, "I can report to my government and my party that the so-called lyric poetry in Leningrad is dead."

The government and party to whom this news was reported was, of course, in Moscow. To understand the re-birth of poetry in Leningrad it is necessary to understand the role of Moscow poetry and Moscow poets in the Soviet literary and political scene. And if, as Alexander Kushner writes, "it is the city that makes the soul" one key to this understanding lies in architecture.

In direct contrast to Leningrad's classical architectural unity, Moscow is now in architectural ferment. Physically, Moscow is a sprawling modern city. And, although the change is being bitterly lamented by its artists, the city's old character is being destroyed in the name of progress. First it was Stalin, who levelled churches to put up parking lots and swimming pools on sites where once stood incomparable works of art constructed by the labour of thousands of Russians. The historic city of "forty times forty churches", of gardens laid out in harmonious rings around circular boulevards, has lost the distinctive beauty of its horizons. Today the skyline is dominated by the looming 30-storey Stalin "wedding cakes" in party-Gothic skyscraper style, and by other skyscrapers which are copies of those in any modern city. Whole blocks of seventeenth- eighteenth- and nine-teenth-century wooden houses, which should have been classified and preserved as historical monuments, have been burned down without a thought to make way for these modern colossi. This is an irreparable loss for the future.

By sacrificing its jewels of the past, Moscow has gained a kind of grey, impersonal face with fewer and fewer surprises and delights for the eye. And, there is about modern Moscow the rootless, transient quality common to many modern cities. Old Moscow was built in wood and wood burns—during its history Moscow has burned more than seventeen times. But this time the change is permanent, irreplaceable. Moscow is now being built in concrete as a kind of monument and showplace to Soviet power.

What is true of the architecture is also true of the soul—and of the language of the soul, poetry. Pre-revolutionary Moscow was primarily a great commercial rather than a cultural centre. After the revolution, in the twenties and thirties, there came to be more and more of an intellectual separation between the artists of Leningrad and those of Moscow. This was as true in art and ballet as in literature. The poetry of Moscow, good or bad, became increasingly a poetry imbued with social consciousness. Poets like Mayakovsky and Yesenin who began in Petrograd became increasingly "Moscow" poets—revolutionary poets, Soviet idealists. The declaiming, dramatic style of the reading of Mayakovsky, exhorting and exciting great audiences, was later continued by Yevtushenko and Voznesensky.

This "social" attitude, the theme of man in his society, which is almost completely absent in Leningrad, persists in the work of the Moscow poets. Today, it is the artists of Moscow who are now close to the seat of power. It is they who, during the past fifteen years, have had international contacts with diplomats and press, they who have occasionally been allowed to travel abroad, they who have become famous. Moscow is after all not only the capital of the Soviet Union but the Mecca of the Soviet Communist Party. There, ideas may be tried on for size in a controlled situation and then, if necessary, quickly rejected. In such a capital, art and politics are close, indeed joined. Thinking and feeling people at all levels, including within the party itself, cannot escape an awareness of the political importance of the artistic side of life. The artist in Moscow is close to the swings and vacillations of policy, close to the top where decisions are made—and changed. When any decision is made, it can only be made in Moscow. It is inescapable that art in Moscow is permeated—albeit often subconsciously—with this preoccupation. A poet who has declaimed before a stadium full of thousands of weeping, cheering people, cannot help but feel himself an influence on the thinking of those who hear him. The party cannot escape considering such a person a potential political influence. The literary magazines of Moscow, *Novy Mir*, *Literaturnaya Gazyeta*, *Ogonyok* are carefully followed for what they reveal of political trends. The loosening of artistic constriction, begun in Moscow under Khrushchev in 1956, was a deliberate political decision. It was the artists of Moscow who were the first scrutinized subjects for the limited experiment in liberalization which the party has since judged to have been unwise.

Relegated to the secondary rank of a provincial city, officially forgotten, Leningrad escaped this sort of attention. The fact that the city was and continues to be controlled by an extremely conservative leadership meant that the easing begun in Moscow came much later to Leningrad. There could be no contacts with foreign press, no publicity; there were no foreign representatives.

There was absolutely nothing an artist could do to influence the leadership. There is no exclusively literary community reserved only for literary and artistic figures comparable in importance and influence to Peredelkino, outside Moscow.

This downgrading of the once proud capital would seem to have made creative life completely hopeless. Yet strangely this imposed isolation has helped the artist in Leningrad to retain a great measure of detachment and independence. These constraining facts of life have served to make the poets of Leningrad more concerned with form and style of language, with the eternal themes of the human soul, life, death, love. Theirs has been an individual rather than a collective search for art. The tradition of individuality is also a Petersburg tradition, one which Anna Akhmatova encouraged among the poets she knew.

The first rip in the thick veil of socialist realism came—inevitably—in Moscow. In 1959, with party permission, Yevgeny Yevtushenko's lyric poetry was published. It was an explosion for the young poets of Leningrad who still say today, "He was our first flag," although since then their enthusiasm for him has dimmed and he is now considered "older". Andrei Voznesensky is admired for his inventive use of language and poetic innovation: "He has the eye of a painter and the ear of a poet." Both are taught in literature classes, but they are considered "very Moscow" with not much connection or direct influence in Leningrad.

At first this change had no immediate effect in Leningrad. Only Victor Sosnora began to be noticed, and at first only in Moscow where he visited and had important friends such as Nikolai Aseev and Lili Brik. But during the early sixties all the major young poets of today's Leningrad began to emerge. They made their first appearances, not in published form, but in informal readings which were permitted and began to attract large followings of listeners among the young technicians, engineers and scientists. Brodsky, a protégé of Akhmatova, was working as a translator and reading his poetry in poetry circles. In 1963 he was judged to be a "parasite", a useless member of society, and sentenced to a five-year period of forced labour. Mercifully, he was released after a year.

As time passed, Sosnora, Gorbovsky and Kushner were published and then became members of the Writers' Union. None of them were yet thirty years old; when Kuzminsky gave his first readings of Byron translations and poetry, Dimitri Bobishev and Yevgeny Rein were also reading. Anatoly Naiman was working on translations of the Italian poet Leopardi and was Akhmatova's literary secretary. Among many others printed for the first time were Leonid Ageev, Vladimir Ufland and Oleg Tarutin. All these poets were then in their twenties.

As it became easier to work and discussions became freer, new groups began to emerge, drawing influence and inspiration from the poetic ideas of the twenties and thirties. Plays were written and produced, painters began to experiment discreetly and to meet with poets. There are today in Leningrad a half-dozen extremely gifted and original young painters, and several novelists and prose writers considered to be of superior talent. All of these artists are virtually unknown outside their own city.

In 1965, Akhmatova was published again. With the intense Leningrad preoccupation with language, there was a revival of interest in the work and ideas of the Russian Futurists—notably Khlebnikov, Kruchenykh and Zabolotsky, as well as the theories of Biely. Annensky and Kuzmin, Bryusov—all found new admirers.

The search at first was not so much for thought as for form. One of the poets said, "The first thing in Leningrad was rhyme—we avoided thought. Our main preoccupation was the Russian literary language. Conservative literary thinking divides thoughts and methods into two different groups. Even the most conservative members of the Union allowed and even encouraged discussion and much variation in the methods of working."

Today there are many variations and "companies" (they do not call themselves "schools", rejecting the implication of stratification in the term). There are neo-Acmeists, of whom the most notable is Kushner. There is a "country" group, influenced by Gorbovsky's work. There are metaphysical poets—among whom Brodsky is the most gifted and important. Brodsky has collected numerous imitators, all influenced also by Pasternak and Mandelstam, and in varying degrees by Akhmatova. There is a company who call themselves "concrete" poets. These are mainly very young poets in their twenties and this concrete poetry is the description of real rather than imaginary objects. And there are "sound" poets, among them Kuzminsky. They are experimenting with language and with pure poetic sound.

These are loosely knit groupings, not at all formally organized. There are endless heated discussions about the merits of one form of poetry or another. One poet of one persuasion will often read to the sceptical members of another and then argue the night away in what seems brutally frank criticism. From time to time, young poets of Moscow or Kiev arrive to read their work, push their views and to listen.

But socialist realism is still pre-eminent. The old party thinkers have been joined by ambitious younger party-minded men. It is difficult, if not impossible, to be published if one is not accepted by the "right" people. One poet was told by an aggressive Young Communist charged with choosing poetry for one of the magazines, "Your verses are fine—only we won't publish them." Astonishingly, the extraordinarily gifted Joseph Brodsky, whose reputation is now world-wide, has yet to have a book published in his own city, although short selections of verses, including "In Memory of T. S. Eliot" were published in *Den Poezii* in 1967 and 1968, and his translations of Polish and Serbian poets have appeared. He lives precariously and is constantly harassed.

It has not been, to date, a totally monolithic negativism. The amount and quality of the work published in *Den Poezii* between 1962 and 1969 did increase. Naturally, the work of the controlling clique appeared with regularity. On the editorial board of selection, along with the well-known names of Dudin, Prokofiev, Sheffner, Braun, Akvilev, Polyakova, and Reshetov have appeared the names of Sosnora in 1966 and Kushner in 1968. In 1968, *Den Poezii* published selections of Akhmatova, Zabolotsky and Kuzmin.

There are group leaders and members of the Writers' Union who, while they do not necessarily agree, do listen to the work of other, differing poets. Natalia Grudinina defended Brodsky at the time of his trial. Vsevelod Rozhdestvensky is a respected old poet who has helped preserve the literary language of the past. Tatiana Gnedich, of the generation of Akhmatova, is a remarkable woman, now seventy, who speaks French and English fluently although she has never left Russia. She spent eleven years in Stalin's prison camps and during a two-year period of solitary confinement she translated from memory whole sections of Byron's *Don Juan* from English into Russian. In recent years, she has finished this massive work and it has been published in the Soviet Union. A respected member of the Writers' Union, she was the leader of a poetry circle in which she listened to the work of young poets, criticized their work and gave them that precious, intangible experience, "culture".

Recently, the hopeful fires of the early and mid–sixties have methodically been banked. Since the fall of 1968 and particularly during the past two years, the atmosphere has tightened. Informal readings in libraries and clubs by unofficial poets have been stopped. Only members of the Writers' Union may now be invited to read.

A major problem is that there are still very few publications in which a poet can be printed. There was a flurry of hope in July 1969, when a new monthly magazine *Aurora* was begun with the stated aim of permitting new writers to print their work. But to date (1971) this magazine has, with only one or two exceptions printed only the work of already established Union poets. In early 1970, a tough and conservative party man, Oleg Shestinsky replaced the respected writer Daniel Granin as head of the Writers' Union.

When Victor Sosnora was accepted by the Writers' Union at the age of 27, he was the youngest member. That was in 1963, and he is still the youngest. For poets who are writing now the road to recognition is difficult indeed. In 1968, a Central Unit for Poetry was established. Under its auspices, Gleb Semeonov headed an important young poetry group, but in the spring of 1970, the group was disbanded and nothing similar has replaced it. The present head of the Poetry Unit, Semyon Botvinnik, is a party conservative in his early forties. He was educated at the University of Moscow and began in the 1950's with translations from old Russian, including the famous *Lay of Igor*. It is he who collects and selects material for the almanacs.

Young poets are now permitted to read their work officially only if invited to do so at the Writers' Union itself, which holds monthly evenings of poetry and music, or in other places, specifically under Union sponsorship. Such invitations are hard to get. First, a poet must be recommended by a member of the Union. Then, his dossier is carefully checked. If he passes these two hurdles successfully, he may then come to audition. Three successive days of readings are held once a year to screen applicants. Of perhaps sixty or seventy who are invited to audition, ten or twelve are accepted as candidates for the monthly readings. To these may be added a few more from important factory and university groups, making a total of perhaps thirty. Of these thirty, only three or four are invited each month. At the end of the year, four or five of the best are selected for a special evening.

One poet was told after his readings at one of these evenings, "Very good, we may permit you to read again in a year or so." Among this new wave of poets, some of great promise and all still in their twenties are: Victor Krivulin, Victor Shira-Li, Oleg Okhapkin, Boris Kuprianov, Tamara Kozlova, Sergei Stratonovsky, Mikhail Gurevich, Victor Toporov and Peter Chegin.

A brief glimpse of their work may occasionally be spotted in one of the literary almanacs. None has yet had a book published, although many of them have been working for years. For all unofficial poets day-to-day survival is a precarious problem. While trying to keep writing and striving to be accepted, they must eke out a living in obscure manual jobs. If they are very lucky they may find translation work to do, but translations take time and careful work and pay irregularly or years after the work is completed. And if they should have the bad luck to remain without work for three months, they risk expulsion from the city.

It is sad that there is no longer any showcase for poetic recitation such as the pre-revolutionary Brodyachaya Sobaka (The Stray Dog), the famous literary club located on The Field of Mars where the artistic elite of Petersburg once gathered. Akhmatova and Kuzmin read there. Mayakovsky, on February 15, 1915, scandalized the audience and all of those "who have a bathroom and a warm W.C." by reciting his poem *Vam* (You There) in which he contrasted the horrors of war at the front with their comfortable life in the capital. The poem ended with the stanza:

> Should I be sacrificing my life
> For you, who love nothing but dames and grub
> I'd rather be serving pineapple soda
> To whores in a bar.

after which ladies fainted and their escorts threatened the poet. The "Stray Dog" was closed by the police in 1915, later reopened and closed again, this time definitively, by the authorities in 1924.

No such prestigious gathering places exist today. But certain cafes have become popular among poets and painters, such places as the Vostok Club, and the Moskva (known locally, for some inexplicable reason as the "Saigon" and also reputed to be a centre for informers). In the summer, one or another beer garden becomes the place to gather and argue. The Food Workers Club three years ago held an evening of Mandelstam. During one such evening of poetry, the discussions became so impassioned that the audience ended the soirée by smashing chairs indiscriminately over each other's heads.

Popular singers use the work of poets as texts for new songs. Gorodnitsky is a popular poet-song writer; the words of Brodsky, Sosnora, and Kuzminsky have been set to music. V. Soloviev-Sedov, perhaps the most famous of Leningrad's song composers (he is the author of the now famous "Moscow Nights" which was originally entitled "Leningrad Nights"), has set the words of Gorbovsky to music. These songs have, on occasion, been broadcast on the radio. "The Gray Horse", a singer's club, became briefly so popular that it was well nigh impossible to obtain tickets for their evenings. Now it, too, has been closed.

And there are still the long magical evenings of the White Nights, which reach their peak from the 18th to the 29th of June. These nights are a festival for the whole city. The Neva's embankments are so crowded that one has to shoulder one's way through crowds at 3 and 4 in the morning. All the young of the city gather night after night to talk, recite, sing and play the guitar.

Poets have always been revered in Russia. Pushkin wrote:

"And I shall long be loved by the people because
I stirred their finer sentiments with my lyre."

Every thinking person knows that there are no easy answers to existence—no nation without problems. To try to deny what is an easily observable fact is not only impractical in the sophisticated modern world, but totally impossible. To continually hear one thing and see another leads inevitably to disbelief and finally cynicism. Slogans can never be enough for a generation who have known from the cradle that life offers no easy way and that flexibility and intelligence are the keys to survival.

Russia today is still a great nation in search of itself. Its greatest asset is, as it has always been, its extraordinary people with their vast reservoir of talent, a people of whom Pushkin said, "It is impossible to rule the Russian people, only to believe in them." They continue to set an example to the world that courage and the search for truth are eternal. No one has yet learned to predict where the spark of spiritual greatness lies. Since no one has learned this, it cannot be extinguished by any disaster as long as there are two men left alive—one to speak and the other to listen.

The five poets in this book are artists, not politicians. They are, if anything, apolitical. Each has an original, entirely individual approach to his art. Products of Soviet society—prevented from knowing any other—nevertheless, they have found and they share with their artistic contemporaries in every country the universal preoccupations of the modern world. There is a strong strain of pacificism in their work—knowing as they do the futility and horrors of war. They hate the ugliness and waste of human values, the pollution of nature, the lack of a sense of beauty in modern life. They are searching, as poets the world over, for meaning in life—their life and the life of their country—for the beauty of nature and the nature of art.

Perhaps the greatest achievement of the Russian Revolution is that it taught millions of people how to read—and so inevitably to think for themselves. These are the audiences, more enthusiastic and involved than any we have in the West in what their own artists are saying. Audiences which are by no means composed of only an intellectual elite, but of working people of all kinds.

If the poets of Leningrad did not accurately reflect the pre-occupations and deepest sensibilities of their listeners, no one would bother to come and hear them. The poets are only the visible, shining tip of an iceberg.

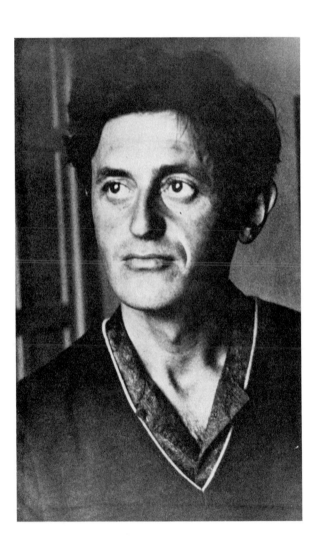

Victor Alexandrovich Sosnora

There is something of a bird in the sharp features of Victor Sosnora, one of those intelligent, surrealistic creatures that live in the world of his poetry. He is taut and spare, with him one is aware not so much of his physical presence as of a hot energy under extraordinary pressure below the surface. This impression is so strong that one feels that his skin must be hot to the touch, or that he could light an electric bulb with his fingers.

His eyes are warm dark brown, almost black, but in some lights they seem to turn a feline yellow. Glowing, knowing, sad—they are the eyes of fever and poetry. They often seem to be attending to some business being transacted in another, invisible world.

Sosnora speaks slowly, almost sleepily. He never raises his voice. His language is clear and pure; he says, "It is my homeland." When he recites his poetry, he raises his eyes to the ceiling, cocks his head slightly back like a bird and pushes out the words in small, intense bursts. His voice becomes warm and increasingly agitated, sometimes breaking with emotion. He is a complex, original loner, rarely mixing, rarely seen. He has no imitators, no disciples, no emotional audiences.

An ultra-sensitive, moody man, Victor Sosnora's melancholy spirit was formed by a dramatic and terrible childhood. Like many people in the Soviet Union, Victor Sosnora is a mixture of races and blood. His father was Polish and Estonian; his paternal grandmother was an Estonian baroness. His mother is Jewish, born in Vitebsk where her father was a rabbi. Before the war, his father and his father's family were a well-known team of acrobats and equilibrists in the Leningrad circus. Although his parents had always lived in Leningrad, his mother believed that her child would be healthier if he started life in the sunshine, so Victor Sosnora was born on April 28, 1936 in Alyupka, Crimea, a small town nestled on the shores of the Black Sea, not far from Yalta.

47

It is a beautiful land of white pebble beaches, snow-capped mountains, blue sea, palm trees, cypresses and flowers. It was a landscape beloved by Pushkin who spent much time in Gurzuf; the Fountains of Bakhschisarai are in the mountains high above.

But his mother's hope was not to be fulfilled. From the age of two to six, he lived in hospitals, suffering from tuberculosis of the bones. There was talk of amputating his hands and feet. The war came. The family team of acrobats was broken up, as it turned out, forever. His father enlisted as a private and was quickly selected for officer's training because of his physical prowess. Two months later he emerged as a second lieutenant and was chosen for a special unit which fought behind the German lines. Of the original 500 members, only he and three or four others survived.

Victor spent two years of the Blockade in Leningrad and suffered, as did all children then, from malnutrition, dystrophy and scurvy. He survived, partly because his mother was then working as an engineer in a metallurgical factory and during the freezing days of the Blockade he was able to live in his mother's office in the factory where he could be kept warm near the stove —the only child among 12,000 workers.

When he was six years old, in the terrible winter of 1942, he was evacuated over the famous Road of Life across the ice of Lake Ladoga, under the strafing of German planes. He was taken to the Kuban, in the south, where he was cared for by his Estonian grandmother, Ulyana. There, he was in great danger from the Gestapo who three times picked him off the streets to be shot as a Jew. Three times his grandmother managed to save him by presenting a forged passport stating that he was her son, and therefore Estonian. Fearing that one day she would come too late, she sent him to live and be protected by a group of partisans whose leader was his uncle, another member of the band of Leningrad acrobats. (This uncle also wrote poetry although very little was ever published.)

Fighting in the steppe, the partisans dug holes under the long grass for protection and cover. Victor was warned never to come out during a battle. He disobeyed and emerged one day to see his uncle and all his band of men shot before his eyes. Victor himself was wounded by an exploding shell and he witnessed the slaughter through a veil of blood drying over his eyes. He was then seven years old. Today on the left side of his face he still bears the scars of that terrible day.

Sosnora's education was sparse and interrupted. His first year of school was in Makhachkala, a small town on the Caspian, his second was in Leningrad. By then, his father was stationed in Warsaw where he was Corps Commander of Polish units which had Soviet Commanding officers. Responsible for 70,000 men, he was deputy to Marshal Rokossovsky. Later he became District Commander in Archangelsk. Victor followed. He lived in Warsaw (1945–6) where he learned Polish which he still reads, in Archangelsk (1946–7) and in Lvov (1948–53). At 19 he entered the army and served from 1956 to 1958 in Leningrad, Archangelsk and Novaya Zemlya. Afterwards he went to work in the same metallurgical factory where he had spent the early part of his childhood. For six years he worked as a labourer on a blast furnace. Although he had begun to write poetry as an adolescent, he began to work seriously only after joining a poetry circle in the factory. In 1959, he briefly joined one of the Gleb Semeonov groups at the Mining Institute. His first verses were published in the Moscow Journal *Literatura i Zhizn* (Literature and Life) in 1960 and then in Leningrad in 1962 in the literary almanac *Molodoy Leningrad* where his work appeared along with Gorbovsky's and Kushner's early verses. His first book *Yanvarsky Liven* (January Showers) was published in Leningrad in 1962. He was helped by his friendship in Moscow with Nikolai Aseev who wrote the preface to his first book, and by Lili Brik, Mayakovsky's great love. In 1963, Sosnora was made the youngest member of the Leningrad Writers' Union. Only then did he leave his work at the factory. His second book *Triptykh* was published in 1965. That same year, in connection with the publication of a French anthology of Russian poetry by the late Elsa Triolet in which several of his poems appeared, he was invited to Paris as part of a delegation of poets which included Boris Slutsky, Andrei Voznesensky, Bella Akhmadulina and Alexander Tvardovsky. He was invited to Paris again in the spring of 1970, where he gave lectures on poetry at the University of Vincennes and the School of Oriental Languages.

Along with his published books of poetry, Sosnora's work often appears in literary journals. His third book of poetry *Vsadniki* (Horsemen) was published in 1969 and a new book of poetry *Aist* (Stork) is scheduled to be published in 1972. He is now finishing a cycle of poems based on tales from Greek mythology. His decision to return to this theme, which has interested many Petersburg poets of the past, stems from his belief that it is a poetic thread which should be reinterpreted by a contemporary poet.

But the interval between published poetry books may stretch to three or even more years, and Sosnora as other poets, must earn his living in other ways. His versatility is extraordinary; he has written novels (none yet published) and plays, criticism for the newspapers, he has worked on documentary films and has written the words to the music of *Hair*, based on a Polish tale. This musical ran in Leningrad in 1969–70. Now he is acting, from time to time, and was considering playing the role of Shakespeare's Henry IV in a Soviet film. He lives for his work and wants few distractions. "My neighbour is always asking me why he hears the typewriter every day. He says, 'It's Sunday, why are you working?' For me, it is life."

Sosnora and his wife Marina, now live in a comfortable apartment which the Union of Writers helped him to obtain. His health is fragile due to his childhood diseases; in the past three or four years he has spent several months in the hospital. He makes several tours a year in the Soviet Union to give readings—to cities in Siberia, Armenia and the far North. Although he is popular with Leningrad audiences, he reads rarely there in public. He is not a gregarious man, he is not easy with people. And he is, it is said, not very popular with some members of the Writers' Union because, says one friend, "He is a lonely wolf. They don't like him because he has more talent, writes better. Then too, he is a very dark and serious man."

In fact, Sosnora is not so much gloomy as hypersensitive and fatalistic. Above all, he is a very gentle man, who has learned to close himself off to people who have so often and so bitterly wounded him. He has a keen intelligence, a curious inquiring mind and an ironic sense of humour. When he is happy and relaxed, a gentle, shy smile lights up in his face, softening the hard lines of disappointment.

Sosnora lives in one of the new apartment districts of Leningrad, almost 45 minutes by taxi from the centre of the city. His apartment is on the 9th—the top—floor, overlooking a vast expanse of horizon broken only by other new apartment buildings and, far off in the distance, mixing the old and new, the gold spires of the Smolny church. There are two rooms—a larger one used as a bedroom-living room and a smaller one used as a study for Victor—plus a kitchen and a bath. Most important, perhaps, it is private; they share it with no one.

Victor's study is bare, with a couch and a table on which rests a typewriter with no casing, so that the keys look strangely disembodied and surrealistic. He is a two-fingered typist, slow and deliberate. He has a small desk with bookshelves, some Mayakovsky, some French books, Hemingway, and a few dictionaries. On the wall, a painting or two by Kulakov, a Leningrad painter who has often done drawings for Victor's poetry books.

In the bedroom-living room there is a fine old Petersburg piano and on it an earthen jug filled with lacy dried grasses. A large portrait of Victor done by Kulakov dominates one corner, a copy of the famous Karsh photographic portrait of Hemingway is pinned on another. There is a little balcony where in the summer there are window boxes filled with vari-coloured daisies, and Victor's striped canvas deckchair.

During the last year, he has acquired a large apricot-coloured poodle, named Runa, whom he lovingly provides with collars and toys.

Upon entering, a visitor is provided with slippers, which Victor bends down and gallantly puts on. When I first met him, it was summer, and he was wearing a bright green cotton shirt and a pair of old khaki cotton pants, on which, with a pen, he had drawn flowers on the knees. In the winter, Victor often wears a sleeveless vest of dark grey shaggy goatskin over his checked flannel shirt. This vest, pungent and marvellously warm, gives him the look of a changeling shepherd. He loves leather and, if he could, would be dressed in leather from head to toe.

One winter evening when it was minus 35 degrees Centigrade outdoors, we ate in the kitchen where it was warm. Marina cooked veal cutlets and potatoes and served them in a brown crock with butter and sour cream. We had lemonade and cognac, then later vodka and oranges. Victor got up and read Pushkin during dinner. Then at dessert they announced that they wanted to sing for me. It was a poem by Pasternak. They sang in duet, Marina in a breathless, little-girl, high-pitched voice, and Victor, ill with grippe, sang off pitch but with profound feeling. Then he read from his own work, standing up, leaning against the wall near the stove, looking at the ceiling, totally absorbed.

Despite his interest in the past, Sosnora is a modern twentieth-century man. In him are the contemporary problems of alienation and loneliness. He is an intellectual without culture, a man who, had he had a university education, might have been a philosopher or an historian. Today, if he could, he would read only history and spend all his time in the archives. Sosnora is a new Soviet phenomenon—a man profoundly troubled by the cataclysms of his childhood and the contradictions of his present. Born like the Soviet Union of mixed bloods and mixed backgrounds, he is curious, seeking, complex, sensitive. Always, there lingers something of the south about him—his voice evokes the melancholy of Jewish laments, his dark hair and black eyes the mystery of the gypsy, the antiquity of the Levant.

Although he has had little formal education, Sosnora has read widely. He reads Polish, knows Ukrainian and a little German ("When I am tired I can speak German like a waterfall"), and has translated Serbian poets into Russian. Of the foreign writers he has read in translation, he likes Dickens' *Pickwick Papers*, Stendhal's *The Red and the Black*, and, especially, Sterne's *Tristram Shandy*. During the past year he has read and admired Faulkner. He emphasizes modestly that he knows nothing of these writers, having read them only in translation. He says he is too lazy to concentrate on learning a foreign language. Above all, his literary interests are Russian. He considers Gogol the greatest Russian prose writer, and like almost all Russian poets cites Pushkin as his greatest master. He read me *The Demons*, his favourite Pushkin poem to illustrate his point. After Pushkin he cites as his great influences Derzhavin, Mayakovsky (he has an excellent collection of early Mayakovsky photographs), then Tsvetayeva, Grigoriev, and Blok, and the fairy tales of Afanasiev.

Sosnora is completely original—in Leningrad, he has no imitators. His early work was full of metallic sounds and images, echoes of his earlier experiences. The *kuznetz* (which means blacksmith, but in modern terms metal worker) has reappeared over and over in different poetic situations. There is still something tangible about his poems; he seems to regard them as a metal worker regards a chunk of steel, something to be bent into shape. In his early poems, his assonances and attitudes sometimes caused his work to be compared with Voznesensky. In one aspect the two have remained similar—their concern for the place of modern man in an increasingly heartless, modern machine-made society—but otherwise they have taken quite different roads.

Sosnora's later work has become much more complex. In *The Living Mirror*, one of a group of poems he calls his Apocalyptic Cycle, written after he had spent two months seriously ill in the hospital, he takes his reader into a hallucinatory world. He has an extraordinary capacity for transporting the reader in and out of a world of the fantastic, and finally anchoring him firmly in reality in the same poem. In *The Living Mirror*, he takes us through his violent dream, only to bring us back to the ordinary beer kiosk on the street corner in Leningrad. *The Owl and the Mouse* is an ironic, modern fairy-tale, which ends with daylight and the blare of the morning radio.

Although Sosnora does not often write directly to his city or about specific scenes there, he is, as are all Leningrad poets, totally imbued with it. *The Owls* must be imagined against the background and architecture of Leningrad—a knowledge which, of course, Sosnora assumes his readers to have. The stone buildings, the river at night, the mystery of the streets and canals—all are there, but for him it is its twentieth-century aspect rather than its eighteenth or nineteenth century look that is dominant. He is urban, cerebral, unsentimental. It is said of him in Leningrad that he writes "with the head, not with the heart."

To express himself Sosnora has often used a world of surreal animals. On the first level, they seem curious, even amusing, but through them, a world of dark symbols emerges. The crow, the raven reappear. He often uses numbers—13 owls, 22 birds, 12 stars, 32 tails, 7 lions, 7 candles—for which he can give no conscious reason: "Only that I think that numbers are at the root of everything." He builds a world around the owls. He uses the familiar language and expressions of Russian fairy tales to heighten the dreamlike atmosphere. Personally he is fond of telling animal fables and stories of strange creatures. "All things in nature," he says, "are wiser than man." He has a patient, mysteriously knowing way with animals. "It is simple," he explains. "It all boils down to knowing a few simple things about their habits. Man is too arrogant. He thinks himself too important. Who is to say that a man is a higher form of nature than a tree?" Once asked where is the secret of life kept, he answered quickly and without hesitation, "in water".

Sosnora knows and loves art, and has read a great deal on the subject. He himself draws well with quick, sure strokes and admires especially the work of Braque, Ucelli and Rembrandt.

During the past two years, as Sosnora has matured, he has become increasingly obsessed with looking for the roots of the Russian past, particularly the Kievan heritage of early Russia. He has been studying Russian *byliny* (tales and sagas) and biblical tales. He started a novel about the eighteenth-century poet Derzhavin, "but then," he says, "I realized it was really about Peter III." This novel is now completed, and he says that if he could afford the time he would now study only history. He has been spending much of his time pouring through historical sources and archives of old Russia. He is an admirer and a heated defender of Peter III, a man whom historians generally dismiss as a feeble, inept ruler. Sosnora views Peter the Great as a fearful personage. *The Thirteen Owls*, he says, are about Peter: "Owls, beloved of Pallas Athena, are a symbol of wisdom, power, authority and fear."

His last volume of verse, *Vsadniki*, written over the past eight years and published in the summer of 1969, is a collection of poems entirely based on old Russian themes, both legendary and historical. From this collection comes the *Tale of the City of Kitezh*. Although based on old themes there is, in these verses, a very bitter, modern, twentieth-century ring. The language is reminiscent of old Russian sagas, but it is also very contemporary, close and personal. He deals with the eternal and useless devastation of war, the destruction of good by violence, the irony of power which conquers only to find that it has conquered skulls and rotting carcasses. The preface to *Vsadniki* was written by Dimitri Likhachev, an Academician, Russia's greatest living authority on ancient and medieval literature and language. This great scholar, now in his sixties, lives in Leningrad, and it is clear that Sosnora has been influenced by his thinking. In his introduction, Likhachev notes that the stark description of war in these poems stems from Sosnora's terrible experiences as a child. He goes on to write that, "The poetic method of Victor Sosnora reproduces, in fact, the fundamental life of his verses. His verses are born from his domination of the familiar, ordinary language. He finds treasures extracted from the entrails of the Russian language. Ideas are born from the very roots of words."

At first, when reading Sosnora, he seems fantastic, at times incomprehensible. Then as his poems are studied and re-read, they sink into the reader's subconscious. From this world of symbols, as through a looking glass, suddenly another world, clear and meaningful, emerges. It is rather the same experience as when one suddenly grasps a foreign language.

Sosnora is a medium, a sort of twentieth-century prophet, who senses in his imagination apocalypses yet unseen by ordinary mortals. His sensitivity to his environment is so acute that when it is out of balance, he is out of balance. He is like an antenna probing the moods and tempers of the invisible. Through his gift, then, is reflected a hallucinatory, poetic world, full of symbols, which, unconsciously, reveals the atmosphere of the real world around him. Does he realize this? I think not. It comes from his extraordinary poetic connection with his country, his city and its moods and feelings. His work, at first bitter-sweet but basically hopeful, full of a kind of rough worker's pride, has become increasingly sombre and despairing.

ROSES

Roses—
burden of eastern poets,
enclosing arabic designs and rhymes.

Roses—
colour of watermelon,
colour of sand,
their petals moving
like the blades of turbines.

Roses—
squirrel fur to the fingers,
and rowan berry to the tongue.

Roses—
varied in temperature,
each in its own way moved by praise,
Yet in their colouring,
as dashing
as a slalom.
Black roses—
black beer,
in goblets of anthracite.
Red roses—
mares backs,
their flanks covered in lather.

Roses—
in every milligram of ink
used by Pushkin, Shelley, Tagore.
But the rose trade
Has become a slave trade

РОЗЫ

Розы —
обуза восточных поэтов,
поработившие рифмы арабов

 и ткани.

Розы —
по цвету арбузы,
по цвету пески,

 лепестками
шевелящие,
как лопастями турбины.

Розы —
меж пальцев — беличья шкурка,
на языке — семя рябины.

Розы
различны по температуре,
по темпераменту славы,
а по расцветке
отважны,
как слалом.
Черные розы —
черное пиво,
каменноугольные бокалы.
Красные розы —
кобыльи спины
со взмыленными боками.

Розы
в любом миллиграмме чернил
Пушкина, Шелли, Тагора.
Но уподобилась
работорговле

Roses—
Peddled for attar
Wholesale!
Oil for pain-killers!
Even roses must pay their way,
and this perhaps is right.
One must have pills for pain,
as well as a still life
livening up the wallpaper.
Fair enough.
Only that one should be concerned
with more than just offspring and tea.
Roses resemble people,
turning sad in the evening.
And in the rose fields
as everywhere, one finds plans and Saturdays.
Roses resemble people,
living just the same sunny,
kind,
brief life.

J. S.

розоторговля.
В розницу розы!
Оптом!
На масло,
в таблетки для нервов!
Нужно же розам
«практическое примененье».
Может,
и правильно это.
Нужны же таблетки от боли,
как натюрморты нужны
для оживленья обоев.
Правильно всё.
Только нужно ведь печься
не только о чадах и чае.

Розы как люди.
Они вечерами печальны.
И на плантациях роз
такие же планы, субботы.
Розы как люди.
С такою же солнечной,
доброй,
короткой судьбою.

SUMMER GARDEN
(The Dream of an Excursionist)

Winter had prepared its approach.
The ground was prepared for frost.
And the circles of the watchers of statues

Grow smaller, ever smaller, and smaller.
I lumber—the last of the great elephants.
A spectator of the statue watchers.
But the statues are strolling around the garden,

> in circles,
> in circles.

I follow them as I am able
But suddenly I feel myself petrifying;
Still chewing a cigarette end
My mouth stiffens skeletally,
and barely stammers:

> "Hey, silhouettes!"

Oh put an end to your processions.
Now, instantly!
Can I escape
your stoniness, your immobility?
But I am turning to stone,
While the statues—

> go on strolling, strolling.

ЛЕТНИЙ САД
(Сон экскурсовода)

Зима приготовилась к старту.
Земля приготовилась к стуже.
И круг посетителей статуй
все у́же, и у́же, и у́же.

Слоняюсь — последний из крупных
слонов —
     лицезрителей статуй.
А статуи ходят по саду
по кругу, по кругу, по кругу.
За ними хожу, как умею.
И чувствую вдруг —
       каменею.
Еще разгрызаю окурки,
но рот костенеет кощеем,
картавит едва:
     — Эй, фигуры!
А ну, прекращайте хождение
немедленным образом!

Мне ли
Не знать вашу каменность, косность.

И всё-таки я — каменею.
А статуи —
    ходят и ходят.

THE LIVING MIRROR

In my room I have a candelabrum—
seven candles, like seven ballerinas in fiery red kerchiefs.
The ballerinas play games,
clink glasses and laugh.
I am a Soviet sultan.

In my room at dusk are seven lions.
The lions are untamed.
They have biblical eyes, and the distance between their fangs
is that between Scylla and Charybdis.

In my room I have gothic and modern swords.
A Lobachevsky would muddle the infinite number of zeroes
enumerating the plebians, the time-servers and anti-heroes
which I have mutilated through the ages, from Granada to
    Jerusalem.
This steel is for duels.

In my room—where is Donna Anna?—there is a statue of the
    Commander
But where is Donna Anna, full of life like an Egyptian woman,
her body quivering and hung with bracelets?
The statue of the Commander, like the ghost in the drama, is the
    masterpiece of some quarry.

But I have placed a small recording machine in the Commander's
    mouth,
so that, at my most crucial moments
he should sound off with some nonsensical and sentimental
    sayings.
I have tamed a large butterfly,
such as no other collector in the world possesses.
She has existed as long as I, even a little longer.
She flutters in
and lands upon my marble window sill.
We discuss things which only she and I know.

ЖИВОЕ ЗЕРКАЛО
1

В комнате у меня канделябр —
семь свечей, как семь балеринок в огненно-красных
платочках.

Балеринки балуются:
чокаются рюмочками и смеются.
Я — советский султан.

В комнате у меня, в сумраке — семь львов.
Львы недрессированы,
у львов библейские очи и расстояние между клыками, как
между Сциллой и Харибдой.

В комнате у меня и готические и современные шпаги.
Любой Лобачевский перепутает энную цифру нулей,
перечисляя плебеев, временщиков и антигероев,
искалеченных мной во все времена, — от Гренады до
Иерусалима.
Эта сталь — для дуэлей.

В комнате у меня — где донна Анна? — статуя Командора.
Где донна Анна, вся живая, вся египтянка, вся в
браслетах, с трепещущим телом?
Статуя Командора, как и драматургический призрак — перл
какой-то каменоломни.

Но в уста Командора я вмонтировал магнитофончик,
чтобы в самый ответственный мой момент
он проповедовал чепуху сентиментальных сентенций.

Я приручил большую бабочку,
которой нет ни у одного коллекционера во всей вселенной.
Она существует столько, сколько я существую и немного
больше.

Она прилетает
и опускается на мраморный мой подоконник.
Мы говорим только о том,
что знаем только она и только я.

She has flown to all the corners of the globe (if a globe can have
    corners)
Disregards the irrelevant,
and knows nothing but secrets.

I have a typewriter.
Actually it is not a typewriter,
but a portable piano.
I touch the keys with my fingertips,
when red sparks flash across the evening sky.
If a room is a miniature of the world,
I would not wish my miniature on anyone.
In my room I have a mirror.

2.

In the evenings, when the gentle embers of the sun
die out in the sky
when the bell of the sea flashes bronze
and eight merry moons
put up their mirrors,—
curtains in green and red scattered patches
on the street imaginary lamp-posts.
At dusk only the fitful flashes of lightning illuminate the room,
then the imperial thunder crashes out, vulgar and terrifying.
Thus it was in times of revolution, like those of Bonaparte and
    Pancho Villa
before an execution twenty-two drums would roll.
And serpentine downpours, like Laocoon's snakes,
are breaking my only window.
The watercolour panes
fall from their frames and fly out diagonally into the vastness of
    the storm.
And through the frames, the bars of my caged world,
trunks of snakes burst into the room.

Она облетела все уголки земного шара (если у шара

могут быть уголки)

Она не знает ничего постороннего,
а то, что знает — только тайна.

У меня есть пишущая машинка.
Собственно говоря, это не пишущая машинка,
а портативное фортепьяно.
Я касаюсь клавиш подушечками пальцев,
когда появляются красные искры на моем вечернем небе.

Если комната — миниатюра мира,
не пожелал бы кому-нибудь моих миниатюр.

В комнате у меня — зеркало.

2

Вечерами, когда угасают на небе
нежные искры солнца,
когда замигает бронзой
вечерний колокол моря,
и восемь веселых лун
расставят свои зеркала, —
занавески в зеленых и красных рассеянных пятнах,
на улице — вымышленные фонари,
в сумерках только молнии освещают комнату

мельканьем, —
тогда вульгарно и страшно гремит государственный гром.
Так во времена бонапартовских и революций Панчо Вильи
перед казнью гремело двадцать два барабана.
И змеиные ливни, как змеи Лаокоона,
рушат мое единственное окно.
Акварельные стекла
выпадают из рам и улетают в пространство грозы по

диагоналям.
И сквозь рамы — решетки моего животного мира —
рушатся в комнату туловища змей.

All seven of my ballerinas tremble with fear.
Melting in tears of candle wax,
their fiery red kerchiefs sink lower and lower
then die out in bronze.

The lions, holding the marble poses of sphinxes
rear up like dogs on their hind legs,
barking like dogs in horror,
fling themselves on their backs
and die, frogs bellies upwards.
Pointless the struggle!
There are too many snakes!

Fight on, fight on, my little moth!
This is the butterfly extending her hidden claws.
   (and the snakes rear up on their tails,
already writhing above my head!)
she swoops down on the snakes,
carries them from the room, like spaghetti out of a pot
and throws them, staggering slightly on her wings, out of the
   window
but, bitten, she collapses somewhere in the darkness and the
   lightning flashes.

In this struggle the Commander remained a pacifist.
The lucky fellow deigned to speak a micro paradox into the
   microphone.
(the air is dark and bright,
and glowing like bengal fires, the carnival bright eyes of snakes,
flew through the room.
Their bodies, like those of Alexandrian courtesans,
were well trained and quivering.
All over the room appeared
snouts of monsters, birds, toads, half-crocodiles.
The snakes stood up and swayed like reeds.)

Балеринки мои — все семь — трепещут от страха.
Они заливаются стеариновыми слезами,
их огненно-красные платочки опускаются ниже и ниже и
                                                угасают в бронзе.

Львы, лежавшие в мраморных позах сфинксов,
встают по-собачьи на задние ноги,
от ужаса лая, как псы,
опрокидываются на спину
и подыхают вверх лягушачьим брюхом.
Бесполезна борьба!
Многое множество змей!

Бейся, бейся, мой мотылек!
Это бабочка выпускает глубоко затаенные когти
                              (а змеи встают на хвосты,
клубятся уже над моей головой!)
налетает на змей,
вынимает из комнаты их, как из чугунка спагетти,
и выбасывает, покачнувшись на крыльях, в окошко,
но, ужаленная, опадает куда-то в темноту и в мелькание
                                                молний.

В этой схватке еще пацифист — Командор.
Сей счастливчик соблаговолил и сказал в микрофон
                              микропарадокс.
(Воздух темен и светел,
и летали по воздуху комнаты
карнавальные очи змей с бенгальским оттенком.
Их тела, как тела александрийских любовниц,
были натренированы и трепетали.
Появлялись повсюду
птичьи, жабьи, полукрокодильи морды чудовищ.
Змеи стояли, как тростники и так же качались.)

Curiously eyeing this airy slithering,
The Commander sighed and said:
"Life is not what it was, nor are we".
Which having said, he disappeared into thin air.

Everything vanished.
Ballerinas extinguished.
Lions devoured.
The whole of my illusory reality
(Composed with such great efforts, butterflies and all)
swallowed up by this storm.
Enraged,
I drew a sword; but . . .
sword after sword melted like icicles,
drops of metal dissolved in drops of rain.

And then, gleaming monotonously, a mirror appeared in the
    semi-darkness.
This mirror had always dimly reflected things,
but now it no longer reflected anything.
And all the snakes
drooped and looked at themselves in the mirror.
And,
hypnotized by their own gaze,
crawled into the jaws of their own reflections,
swallowing themselves.

Good morning, Comrade!
Thank you for saving me!
All happened, as all brilliant things do, simply.
The mirror will have soon digested them:
ballerinas and lions, monsters and dawn,
and will again go back to its normal state of reflecting objects.
Every nightmare will dissolve.
You will enter it with your electric shaver,
In the mirror you are just your everyday double.
And you will start cleverly and with clever eyes
to tool the stubble—
the details of your everyday and identical face.

И с любопытством рассматривая воздушное пресмыканье,
Командор вздохнул и сказал:
— И жизнь уже не та, и мы уже не те.
Он сказал и пропал в пустоте.

Все пропало.
Балеринки погасли.
Львов съели.
Всю мою иллюзорную современность
(я с такими усилиями и с бабочками ее сочинял)
поглотила и эта гроза.
Взбешенный,
я выхватил шпагу, но...
шпага за шпагой, как сосульки, таяли капля за каплей,
капли металла растворялись в каплях дождя.

И тогда, монотонно сверкая, появилось зеркало из
                                        полутьмы.
Это зеркало смутно кое-что отражало,
но когда появилось, перестало что бы то ни было отражать.
И все змеи опустились,
оглянулись на зеркало и посмотрели.
И,
загипнотизированные собственным взглядом,
они вползали в пасти собственных отражений,
пожирая сами себя.

С добрым утром, товарищ!
                        Спасибо тебе за спасенье!
Все случилось, как все гениальное, просто.
Скоро зеркало все переварит:
балеринок и львов, и чудовищ твоих и рассвет,
и займется опять естественным отраженьем предметов.
Улетучится каждый кошмар.
Ты войдешь с электрической бритвой,
ты и в зеркале твой повседневный двойник.
И вы станете умно и с умными глазами
фрезеровать волосинки —
детальки своих повседневных и одинаковых лиц.

Good morning!
Still only half a sun and half a sky,
but in time there will be a whole sun, a whole sky.
The main thing is to stand firm, friend!
I fell down on my knees and wept,
a pilgrim in the half-dark deserts of the house of Damocles
Myself a Creator, I prayed to the invisible Creator.

3.
I was tired today,
and I shall not get through tomorrow.
I am not asking for forgiveness,
but, Lord, asking simply:
that everything stay as it is:
the sunny reality
of prisons, barracks and hospitals.

If I weary
of prisons, barracks and hospitals
in the totalitarian theatre of the absurd,
if my hand of its own accord
raises up against me some tool of liberation,
stay it, Lord, and force it down.

Let everything stay as it is:
the prison cells of the plebs,
wild drumbeats,
the convulsions of operating tables,
and everything by which man lives,—
dried fish,
brackish water,
a salt lick
Give me a Judas, I pray you, in my Garden of Gethsemane!

С добрым утром!
Еще полусолнышко и полунебо,
но со временем будет Солнце и Небо,
только выстоять нужно, дружок!
Я стоял на коленях и плакал,
пилигрим в полутемной пустыне

дома Дамокла.
Сам Творец, я молился невидимому Творцу.

3

— Я сегодня устал,
а до завтра мне не добраться.
Я не прощенья прошу,
а, Господи, просто прошу:
пусть все, как есть, и останется:
солнечная современность
тюрем, казарм и больниц.

Если устану
от тюрем, казарм и больниц
в тоталитарном театре абсурда,
если рука сама по себе на меня
поднимет какое орудье освобожденья, —
останови ее, Господи, и опусти.

Пусть все, как есть и останется:
камеры плебса,
бешеные барабаны,
конвульсии коек операционных,
и все, чем жив человек, —
рыбу сухую,
болотную воду
да камешек соли
дай мне Иуду, молю, в саду Гефсиманском моем!

If I should die,—
who will devise a sunny reality
in the world,
where to me alone it has been given
merely to invent, not to live.
I shall not touch the goods and riches of thy creatures.
I do not even have disciples.

Only in the fairy tales of my grandmother Ulyana,
have I known a few patches of sunlight,
more than this I have not known,
if it must be thus,—
then for more I will not ask,
                              I swear!
Do not preserve me Lord,
as a human creature,
but keep me
as your instrument.

4.
In the mornings there is emptiness.
From fear, with trembling heart
I drink a beer at a street stand:
It is the Day of Judgment, the Last Day.

Plain people weep from beer.
There is a lot of beer, and not enough tears for it all.
Their nails are like cracked marble,
And on their faces there is nothing, only their troubles
smiling from somewhere around the corner.

So what. On this Day, my Last,
everyone should be just a little sad,
so to speak, tipsily sad.

Если умру я, —
кто сочинит солнечную современность
в мире,
где мне одному отпущено
лишь сочинять, но не жить.
Я не коснусь всех благ и богатств твоих тварей.
Нет у меня даже учеников.

Только что в сказках бабки Ульяны
знал я несколько пятнышек солнца,
больше — не знал,
если так надо, —
больше не буду,
                    клянусь!
Не береги меня, Господи,
как тварь человечью,
но береги меня,
как свой инструмент. —

4

По утрам пустота.
И от стража с трепещущим сердцем
я стою у пивного ларька:

Судный День, День Последний.
Простолюдины плачут от пива.
Пива много, и на все пиво их слез слишком мало.
Ногти у них, как в трещинках мрамор.
И на лицах у них — ничегошеньки, кроме где-то из-за угла
                              улыбающейся тоски

Что ж. В этот День, в мой Последний,
все должны быть немножко грустны,
так сказать, грустны навеселе.

73

LETTER

Oh, remember me in your garden
where ants with red shields lived
and where the large sparrows unfolded
their petals like lilies.

Oh, remember me in your land
where birds flew in a warm world,
and where on a spire a golden angel
always tried to fly south—but could not.

Oh, remember me in your garden,
where the bells' fruits ring
like a funeral knell
                              and spiders
weave the meridians of their webs.

Oh, remember me in your tears
where the white nights are like shackles
and where castles of blue uniforms
will guard you every night.

ПИСЬМО

О вспомни обо мне в своем саду,
где с красными щитами муравьи,
где щедро распустили лепестки
как лилии, большие воробьи.

О вспомни обо мне в своей стране,
где птицы улетели в теплый мир,
и где со шпиля ангел золотой
все улетал на юг... и не сумел.

О вспомни обо мне в своем саду,
где колокольные звонят плоды,
как погребальные,
                                        а пауки
плетут меридианы паутин.

О вспомни обо мне в своих слезах,
где ночи белые, как кандалы,
и где дворцы в мундирах голубых
тебя ежевечерне стерегут.

IN YOUR EYES

In your eyes, in your snows
I, unhappy wayfarer, freeze
No, I was not muddled—not mistaken:
in your eyes I—am your Susanin.

In your desperate snows
White strumming of a guitar.
I am your soldier, not servant,
composer of a bright farewell.

Oceans of evil will engulf us . . .
Oh, do not threaten, do not threaten,
I am your soldier, your salute,
eyes, inextinguishable as the sky.

What sort of pleasure there, to hell with it!
We only recognized the melody
of how youth has gone,
of how, perhaps, we are tired.

В ТВОИХ ОЧАХ, В ТВОИХ СНЕГАХ

В твоих очах, в твоих снегах
я, путник бедный, замерзаю.
Нет, не напутал я, — солгал:
В твоих очах я — твой Сусанин.

В твоих отчаянных снегах
гитары белое бренчанье.
Я твой солдат, но не слуга,
слагатель светлого прощанья.

Нас океаны зла зальют...
О не грози мне, не грози мне.
Я твой солдат, я твой салют,
очей, как небо, негасимых.

Каких там, к дьяволу, услад!
Мы лишь мелодию узнали
про то, как молодость ушла,
про то, как, может быть, устали...

Six Selections from

THE THIRTEEN OWLS

THE CONTOURS OF THE OWL

Midnight flowed secretly as the sap of birch trees.
Policemen stiffened like fingers on street corners.
Only shepherd dogs clinked their chains before the buildings,
moving their tails like the microbes of cholera.
Deep sleep. Buildings somnolent as the work of a dramatist
for whom reality is banished from his pages.
Three million curtains keep reality at bay.
Three million lampshades heighten somnolence.
But on the chimneys and the drainpipes,
on the park-hedges, the balustrades and aerials,
everywhere perched the owls.
They are the owls, they are the owls!
I know those haughty shapes!
In fearful, fur-covered coats—they are the owls!
They part their bony lips and smile with arrogance,
illuminating the depths of the city with their snow-white eyes.
Oh my city! Oh Tsarina!
torn by the beaks of owls grinning like pikes,
these birds blaspheme over your captive, naked body
in the glow of their white, insolent eyes.
Oh my city! Captive city!

КОНТУРЫ СОВЫ

Полночь протекала тайно,
                              как березовые соки.
Полицейские, как пальцы,
                              цепенели на углах.
Только цокали овчарки
                    около фронтонов зданий
да хвостами шевелили, как холерные бациллы.
Дрема. Здания дремучи,
                         как страницы драматурга
у которого действительность
                            за гранями страниц.
Три миллиона занавесок
                         загораживало действо.
Три миллиона абажуров нагнетало дрему.
Но зато на трубах зданий,
                         на вершинах водосточных
труб,
на изгородях парков,
                    на перилах, на антеннах —
всюду восседали совы.
Это совы, это совы!
                    узнаю кичливый контур!
В жутких шубах, опереньем наизнанку, —
                                        это совы!
улыбаются надменно, раздвигая костяные
губы,
озаряя недра зданий снежнобелыми глазами.
Город мой! Моя царица,
                    исцарапанная клювом

But someone stands upon the central square,
bald and in oil-skins, like the tsar's statue,
with furrowed brows, his bald head blazing red,
his hands pressed to his head like ears.
He seems to be surrendering, his hands already raised,
he is captive, a huge torch, a steel worker or blacksmith;
but in reality all was much simpler:
he had not even seen the birds.
He was smiling gently at the melodies of his hands,
five stringed musical instruments.

J. S.

сов,
оскаленных по-щучьи,
ты — плененная, нагая
и кощунствуют над телом эти птицы,
озаряя
снежнобелыми и наглыми глазами.
Город мой! Плененный город!
Но на площади центральной
кто-то лысый и в брезенте,
будто памятник царю,
он стоял, — морщины-щели, —
алой лысиной пылая,
и ладони, будто уши, прислоняя к голове.
И казалось — он сдается,
он уже приподнял руки,
он пленен,
огромный факел,
сталевар, или кузнец.
А на деле было проще:
он и не глядел на птицу,
медленно он улыбался под мелодии ладоней —
пятиструнных музыкальных инструментов!

THE EYES OF THE OWL AND ITS TERROR

On an antenna, like an anchorite
You have perched, owl.
In this neighbourhood (this narrow gorge!)
there are no visitors, no loiterers.

You have perched, huge
my sorrow, my storm.
How they blaze,
               the approaching
snow white eyes.

Snow white like lookouts
on black hulled ships
The bird this midnight—is enslaved.

You are frightened? Afraid?
A hundred times disillusioned?
But gaze: in the eyes of the beast,
snow white—
            there is also terror.

ГЛАЗА СОВЫ И ЕЕ СТРАХ

На антенне, как отшельница,
взгромоздилась ты, сова.
В том квартале (в том ущелье!)
ни визитов, ни зевак.

Взгромоздилась пребольшая
грусть моя, моя гроза.

Как пылают,

          приближаясь,
снежно-белые глаза.
Снежнобелые, как стражи
чернокожих кораблей.
Птица полуночной страсти
в эту полночь — в кабале.

Ты напуган? Розовеешь?
Разуверенный стократ?
Но гляди: в глазах у зверя
снежнобелый —

          тоже страх.

THE FOOTSTEPS OF THE OWL AND ITS LAMENT

Left-right! Left-right!
Along the pavement marches an owl,
                    clad in rectangular cardboard cloak.
                    A bronze trident on its shoulders rings.
                    Passing the courtyards—caverns of wood—
                    with raucous guffaw, the owl goes.

Left-right-left-right!
Along the pavement sidles an owl.
                    Millionaire and beggar—take care!
                    Bard who spouts his anthems out!
                    The owl on his trident will prong you all
                    like macaroni on a fork.

Left! Right! Left! Right!
Along the pavement swaggers the owl.
                    Crawl to escape . . . Too late! The kill!
                    It pecks out the liver: out to smash
                    collarbones; sucking—sucking scabs;
                    plunges syringe—syringe of its bill.

Left . . . right . . . left . . . right . . .
Along the pavement hollers the owl,
                    in quiet and darkness, sobbing, black
                    as tar. Enormous teardrops well
                    on tiptoe up, enkindling its big
                    toe (as a candle tips flame . . .)

                                                    P. R.

ШАГИ СОВЫ И ЕЕ ПЛАЧ

Раз-два! Раз-два!
По тротуарам шагает сова.
        В прямоугольном картонном плаще,
        медный трезубец звенит на плече,
        мимо дворов — деревянных пещер —
        ходит сова и хохочет.
Раз-два-раз-два!
По тротуарам крадется сова.
        Миллионер и бедняк! — не зевай!
        Бард, изрыгающий гимны-слова!
        Всех на трезубец нанижет сова,
        как макароны на вилку!
Раз! Два! Раз! Два!
На тротуарах ликует сова!
        Ты уползаешь? Поздно! Добит!
        Печень клюет, ключицы дробит,
        шрамы высасывая, долбит
        клювом, — как шприцем, как шприцем.
Раз... два... раз... два...
На тротуарах рыдает сова.
        В тихом и темном рыданье — ни зги.
        Слезы большие встают на носки.
        Вот указательный палец ноги
        (будто свечу, зажигает...)

The great bronze, equestrian statue of Peter the Great erected by
Catherine the Great on the bank of the Neva river became the
subject of one of Pushkin's most famous poems, *The Bronze
Horseman*. In it, one moonlit night the statue comes alive and
gallops through the city in pursuit of a young, helpless Russian.
In Sosnora's poem, the owl, symbol of authority, becomes the
horseman.

THE BRONZE OWL

Slowly a horseman through the town
galloped with hooves that rang like glass.
Its pupil blazed—an icy white
bullseye, pale in a ghoul-green face.

Ikon—I see and I know Thee, Sire!
In feathered soutane—how beauteous!
Thine is the city—to thee the port
reports—holy Peter, helmsman owl.

From brains of bronze, from lips of brass,
corrosion of blood on a bronze moustache.

A droplet of blood goes sliding down,
hangs on his nose tomato-like.
Fanatic, rejoice, O monster cruel!
I offer my cheeks to you in a bowl.

I'm bald as a mongol, a brainless skull,
yet you are undone, while I, my monster,
                    am yet to be!
I am the terrible builder, guardian of gates;
some day my star will strike, will soar,

МЕДНАЯ СОВА

По городу медленно всадник скакал.
Копыто позванивало, как стакан.
Зрачок полыхал — снежнобелая цель
на бледнозеленом лице.

Икона! Тебя узнаю, государь!
В пернатой сутане сова — красота!
Твой город! Тебе — рапортующий порт!
Ты — боцман Сова, помазанник Петр!

Из меди мозги, из меди уста,
коррозия крови на медных усах.

И капля из крови направлена вниз, —
висит помидориной на носу.
Ликуй, истеричка, изверг, садист!
Я щеки тебе на блюдце несу!

Я гол, как монгол, как череп, безмозгл.
Но ты-то скончался, я — буду, мой монстр!
Я страшный строитель, я стражник застав.
Когда-то моя прозвенит звезда,

vertically transfixing Peter.
Then you'll be plucked—feathers and all.

     ★   ★   ★

Giant horses carry Russia along,
squiggles of owlish dogma beneath,
Byzantine owlish ikons beneath
And a tiny, tin horse.

P. R.

она вертикалью вонзится в Петра! —
ни пуха, ни пера!

———————————

А кони-гиганты Россию несут,
а контуры догмы совиной — внизу,
внизу византийство совиных икон
и маленький, металлический конь.

THE OWL AND THE MOUSE

Once upon a time there was a roof, covered with tin.
From rust
the tin was as fluffy as the fur of a puppy's coat.
Once upon a time on the roof was a chimney.
It was black and terrifying
as a policeman's inkwell.
The chimney stood at attention
like a coward before a generalissimo.
But in the apartments already many ages ago
steam heat had been installed.
So that the chimney, as it proved,
stood uselessly—
a forgotten architectural excess.
And as no stoves were lit,
from the chimney no smoke came.
And in order to make up for this serious omission,
exactly at midnight,
when the clock struck twelve times
(actually the clock did not strike at all,
because in the house,
already ages ago,
the old chiming clock had been destroyed;
in the house now, there were alarm clocks;
so there was no clock,
but. . . .
just as adults read books not aloud, but to themselves,
thus it seemed to the children
that the clock struck all the same, at midnight
as in their fairy tales, not aloud, but to itself;
so it seemed to the children,
although they, at twelve o'clock at night were already sound
    asleep.
because children retire to bed earlier
very different from adults,

СОВА И МЫШЬ

Жила-была крыша, крытая жестью.
От ржавчины
жесть была пушистая, как шерсть щенка.
Жила-была на крыше труба.
Она была страшная и черная,
как чернильница полицейского.
Труба стояла навытяжку,
как трус перед генералиссимусом.
А в квартирах уже много веков назад
укоренилось паровое отопление.
Так что труба, оказывается,
стояла без пользы —
позабытое архитектурное излишество.
Так как печи не протапливались,
то из трубы не вылетал никакой дым.
Чтобы как-то наверстать это серьезное упущенье,
ровно в полночь,
когда часы отбивали двенадцать ударов
(и совсем не отбивали удары часы,
потому что в доме
уже много веков назад
разрушили старинные часы с боем;
в доме теперь были будильники;
значит, часы не били,
но...
как взрослые читают книги не вслух, а про себя,
так и детям мерещилось,
что часы все-таки отбивают в полночь
свои сказочные двенадцать ударов,
и часы отбивают их тоже не вслух, а про себя;
так мерещилось детям,
хотя они в двенадцать часов ночи уже беспробудно спали,
потому что дети укладываются спать пораньше
в отличие от взрослых,

the majority of whom
spend their evenings cogitating the problems of the universe
and only come to the end of these and similar reflections
long after midnight),
now then:
at the very moment when the clock struck twelve times
from the chimney, out flew a cat.
He flew out like smoke, or instead of smoke
and just like smoke, blue.
He flew out and dissolved against the background of the starry
    sky.
At this very same moment a mouse came running across the roof.
The mouse was enormous—large as any sheepdog of any con-
    tinent.

The mouse was shaggy, as all the aforementioned sheepdogs,
and like a sheepdog, shaking itself after a swim.
In the place of a tail, the mouse had a black tooth projecting,
and instead of teeth, from its mouth
projected 32 tails, long and bare.
The tails were as long as human arms,
but they were thicker, and some had fingers and some were
    without.
The tails undulated like snakes.
And on the chimney sat an owl.
It was tiny as a brooch.

—How do you do!—
the huge mouse mumbled obsequiously to the tiny owl.
—Greetings—gruffed the owl.
—It is midnight already, explained the mouse.
—How clever of you to guess, said the owl in mock amazement
it would never have occurred to me that it was already mid-
    night!
The mouse did not understand the humour.
It explained to the owl why it was now midnight, and not earlier,

большинство которых по вечерам
приступают к размышленьям о проблемах вселенной
и заканчивают эти и подобные им размышленья
далеко за полночь),
итак:
в тот момент, когда часы отбивали двенадцать раз, —
из трубы вылетал кот.
Он вылетал, как дым, или вместо дыма,
и такой же, как дым, голубой.
Он вылетал и таял на фоне звездного неба.

Как раз в этот момент по крыше пробегала мышь.
Мышь была огромна — величиной с овчарку всех
                                                континентов.
Мышь была лохмата, как и все выше перечисленные
                                                овчарки,
как овчарка, отряхивающаяся после купанья.
На месте хвоста у мыши торчал черный зуб,
а вместо зубов изо рта
торчали 32 хвоста, длинных и оголенных.
Хвосты по длине равнялись человеческой руке,
но были толще и то с пальцами, то без пальцев.
Хвосты поднимались и опускались, как змеи.

А на трубе сидела сова.
Она была крошечная, как брошка.

— Здравствуй! —
        подобострастно лепетала огромная мышь крошечной
сове.

— Привет... — бурчала сова.
— Уже полночь, — объясняла мышь.
— Какая ты догадливая, — изумлялась сова, —
мне бы никогда не додуматься, что уже полночь!
Мышь не понимала юмора.
Она объясняла сове, почему сейчас полночь, а не раньше,

obsequiously clinking
the chain of its own reasoning.
—Your reasoning is too complicated for my way of looking at the
world, the owl yawned,
—Let's talk about food,—

And the owl greedily surveyed the huge mouse.
Now it is well known,
the basic food of owls consists of rodents.
—No, no, the mouse hastened to reply.
It looked apprehensively at the owl,
swaying the 32 tails projecting from its mouth.
—No, no, better to speak
about the international situation.
—Nonsense, yawned the owl,
among internationals, food is also a situation.
—Let's talk about film art! squirmed the mouse,
—How did you like the extraordinary Latest Film!
—Nonsense! The latest film is baloney! said the owl beginning
to lose its patience.
And at the thought of baloney, its mouth watered.
—What do you think is the origin of the word "mouse"? blurted
   the mouse.
—Well, what is it? the owl inquired languidly.
—It comes from the Latin, "mussiamus".
—Nonsense, lisped the owl. The word mouse comes from the
   word "mouthseful".

It was beginning to get light.
The janitor awoke. The janitor was a woman.
She had a Tartar face—as many do.
She lit a pipe.
Sparks flew out of the pipe like flashes of lightning.
A broom, or a mop flashed through the air and disappeared.

At that very moment the clock struck six.
And when the clock struck,

подобострастно позванивая
цепью своих собственных умозаключений.
— Твои умозаключения очень сложны
для моего восприятия мира, — зевнула сова, —
давай побеседуем о пище, —
и сова алчно осмотрела огромную мышь.
Ведь всем хорошо известно,
что основная пища сов — грызуны.
— Нет, нет, — заторопилась мышь.
Она опасливо поглядывала на сову,
покачивая своими 32 хвостами, торчащими изо рта.
— Нет, нет, лучше мы побеседуем
о международном положенье.
— Чепуха, — зевнула сова, —
между народами тоже положена пища.
— Давай поговорим о киноискусстве! —
закрутилась мышь, —
как тебе нравится изумительный Последний Фильм?
— Чепуха! Последний Фильм — чушь гороховая! —
начала гневаться сова,
и, вспомнив о горохе, облизнулась.
— Как ты думаешь, откуда произошло слово «мышь»? —
выпалила мышь.
— Откуда? — вяло поинтересовалась сова.
— От мыш-ления.
— Чепуха! — отрицательно захохотала сова. — Слово
                                    «мышь» произош
ло от «выкормыш». Вы — корм, мышь!

Стало светать.
Проснулся дворник. Дворник — женщина.
У нее было татарское, как и у многих, лицо.
Она закурила трубку.
Искры вылетали из трубки, подобно молниям.
Блеснула и куда-то пропала метла, или швабра.

Как раз в этот момент часы пробили шесть раз.
А когда часы столько пробили,

Then the owl began rapidly to increase in size,
and the mouse to shrink.
Within a few seconds the owl had grown frigate-sized
and the mouse had shrunk to the size of a little finger.
The owl was jubilant:
now it would gobble up the mouse without any further
conversation.
The feathers bristled on the face of the owl.
But the owl had by now become so large,
that it was unable to see any mouse at all.
The owl sat,
hungry eyes spinning angrily.
It seemed as though two bicycle wheels were spinning
with flashing spokes.
None of the inhabitants of the building had any idea,
that each night on their remarkable roof,
the scene described by me, took place.
A ludicrous scene!
Why, when the mouse is as large as a sheepdog,
doesn't it get the idea to gobble up the owl?
Why doesn't the tomcat pay attention to the mouse?
These are questions that can be deciphered only by the children
    of my country.
When the clock struck the sixth time,
the cat, which had dissolved against the background of the starry
    sky,
gathered its body together drop by drop like a cloud,
condensed,
and blue, flew back into the chimney.

And several million radios,
installed in the bowels of the buildings,
blared in a single uplifting sound
—Good morning to you, Comrades!

тогда сова стала быстро увеличиваться в размерах,
а мышь уменьшаться.
Через несколько секунд сова достигла размеров фрегата,
а мышь уменьшилась до размеров мизинца.
Сова торжествовала:
теперь она сожрет мышь безо всяких там собеседований.
Перья топорщились на лице совы.
Но сова уже стала настолько велика,
что ей уже не видна была никакая мышь.
Сова сидела,
гневно вращая голодными глазами.
Казалось, что это вращаются, пылая спицами,
два велосипедных колеса.
Никто из жителей здания не догадывался,
что каждую ночь на их замечательной крыше
происходит сцена, изображенная мной.
Нелепая сцена!
Почему, когда мышь бывает огромной, как овчарка,
почему у нее не появляется замысла сожрать сову?
Почему кот не обращает внимания на мышь?
В этом способны разобраться лишь дети моей страны.

Когда часы отбивают шестой раз,
то кот, растаявший на фоне звездного неба,
собирал свое тело по каплям, как туча,
сгущался,
и, синий, влетал обратно в трубу.

А несколько миллионов радиоприемников,
размещенных в недрах здания,
выговаривали единым, жизнеутверждающим голосом:
— С добрым утром, товарищи!

WHY WEEPS THE GREAT HORNED OWL

Why weeps the Great Horned Owl?

Because there is no heaven,
Because the darkness holds only
twelve stars, no more.

The twelve stars move,
playing a game,
the mouse swallows the moon
and the raven pecks it.

The raven has made off with time
beyond joy's seven dwellings,
only in the emptiness cries
alone, as always, the Great Horned Owl.

Why weeps the Great Horned Owl?

Because the world has grown small for weeping
because the world is full of mice,
all the stars, only chains.

When the moon was snuffed out
and the sun melting,
and the air was as light
as dandelion thistledown,

when across the sky
the red horse ran
and twenty-two birds
of daylight laughed . . .

that the owl had cried so,
that all those owlish tears—
sleepless, impotent,
were nothing more than that.

О ЧЕМ ПЛАЧЕТ ФИЛИН

О чем плачет филин?

О том, что нет неба,
что в темноте только
двенадцать звезд, что ли.

Двенадцать звезд ходят,
игру играют,
что месяц мышь съела,
склевал его ворон.

Унес ворон время
за семь царств счастья,
лишь в пустоте плачет
один, как есть, филин.

О чем плачет филин?

Что мир мал плачу,
что на земле мыши,
все звезды лишь цепи.

Когда погас месяц
и таяло солнце,
и воздух воздушен
был, как одуванчик,

когда во все небо
скакал конь красный
и двадцать две птицы
дневных смеялись...

что так плакал филин,
что весь плач птичий —
бессилье бессонниц,
ни больше, ни меньше.

Note

Kitezh is a legendary town often mentioned in Russian popular tales and epics. According to these old stories, during the thirteenth-century Mongol invasion, rather than submit to worldly degradation and corruption, the heroic city chose to sink to the bottom of a lake. Under the water, the stories ran, lay a purer existence than that which was found on land. It was said that during the summer solstice a chosen few could sometimes hear the ringing of the bells from its vanished churches and see the lights of the lost city burning beneath the waters.

THE TALE OF THE CITY OF KITEZH

And I shall make my way back to Kitezh, that city where I was
    brought up.
Then I shall dive to the dark depths whose guardians swing the
    gates,
and this return will be thought of as hostile by the guards,
and worthy of suspicion.
I shall go to my wife, to the halls of my dwelling, speaking
"What of my herds?"
                    "The guards have slaughtered them and used
                    the hides for shoe-leather."
Speaking, "What of our son?"
                    "The guards killed him, his body quartered."
Speaking, "What of our daughter?"
                    "Ten times ten guards and forty raped your
                    daughter."
And I shall ask my wife, "What of you?" "What of my liegemen
    and retainers?"
and she will say, "Your servants kept their peace,
and fearing suspicion, your liegemen joined the guards.
As for myself—I am wed to the ruler."

СКАЗАНИЕ О ГРАДЕ КИТЕЖЕ

И я вернусь в тот город Китеж,
туда, где вырос.
Нырну в тот омут, где ворота
вращает стража.
И возвращение мое
расценит стража
как вражью вылазку,

                возьмет
на подозренье.

И я приду к своей жене,
в хоромы храма.
— Где скот? — спрошу я.

           — Сожрала стража,
           на обувь шкуры.
— Где сын? — спрошу я.

           — Убила стража,
           четвертовала.
— Где дочь? — спрошу я.

           — Три смены стражи,
           сто сорок стражей
           твою насиловали дочь
           поочередно.
— А ты? — спрошу я
жену. —
А челядь?..
А побратимы?..
— Молчала челядь, — жена ответит, —
а побратимы
вступили в стражу, во избежанье
подозрений,
я вышла замуж за самодержца, —
жена ответит.

Thus will I turn back to Kitezh which I ruled in the past,
where my servants and liegemen held the walls
and the Mongols could take neither us nor our city,
where every first man was a hero, and every second man
    immortal.

I spoke these words: "Sword-bondsmen, speak the truth:
Are we to give our freedom to the foe, or must we sink?"
Then we roasted alive ten times a hundred hundred bulls
and many times this number of protesting boars
and when the last carcass was burnt, the crawling smoke obscured
    the sun.
Then we sank down at midnight. To the bottom. Utterly.
There remained only cranberry bogs and the songs of serfs,
serf-songs of the immortal City of Heroes.

So I must turn back to Kitezh, to that City of Heroes.
How time has changed the servants of my realm!
The deep ends of the marshes hold no lights.
The days have gone wan. The mares do not neigh.
No grain is harvested, no meat is roasted.
Their noses are like twigs, spineless, blunt as the snouts of fish,
the scimitar shaped whiskers ossified,
human jaw bones collapsed into toad's cheeks:
Thus have my realm's servants changed.

Yet I must turn back to Kitezh, there where loyalty
was once held high as the grain deities.
No one awaits me in that city; he who awaited played me false.
I shall take with me the heads of twelve onions,
which will make up thirteen with my own head.
It seems that in this age the onion
is the last growth which will bring tears.

Then shall I come to the Overlord, speaking
                "Are you truly supreme? Do you rule all?"
                "The guard alone is supreme

Так я вернусь в тот город Китеж,
туда, где правил,
где заправляла делами челядь
и побратимы.
И не могли они, монголы,
сдолать наш город,
где каждый первый — герой,

                          где каждый

второй — бессмертен.

Я обратился:
— Побратимы,
давай по правде:
сдадим поборникам свободу
или потонем? —
И мы зажарили живьем
быков сто тысяч!
Еще визжащих кабанов
сто сотен тысяч!
Последний скот
последовал
таким исчадьем,
что солнце ползало по небу
двумя клопами!
Мы затонули в полночь. Полностью. До нитки.
Остались только кляксы клюквы
да песни смердов,
да песни смердов
про бессмертный
Град Героев.

Вот я вернусь в тот город Китеж,
в тот Град Героев.
Как видоизменилась челядь
моей державы!
Ни огонька на дне болота.
Дни побледнели.

And I rule a little myself. I have, in a way,
the people's support—dictated by the guards."

And I shall leave upon the square—let them weep for a while
my onion, this simple remembrance of nature,
in this land, ruled for centuries by optimism,
where all was transient
where for the slightest tear heads were removed like shoes,
where for the slightest tear heads were sliced off like warts
the guards cried! The people cried, all of them!
The Overlord himself, a mighty ruler with a star upon his chest,
swallowed tears instead of spittle and flew into a rage.
And yet they did not overlook my execution,
or to bury the twelve onion heads in the nearest pit.

Sometime, after, much, much later,
twelve onion heads will sprout over the city
and my head will sprout up as well, a warning
that mine was not to be the last beheading.

But it is said no one has ever seen the city of Kitezh.
That may well be so, no one has seen it.
Indeed, that may well be.

J. S.

Не ржут кобылы.
Не режут злаки.
Не жарят жир.
Носы, торчащие, как сучья,
хрящи прогнули
и окончательно скурносились
по-рыбьи,
луноподобные усы
окостенели,
как будто человечья челюсть,
но жабьи жабры:
так видоизменилась челядь
моей державы.
Но я вернусь в тот город Китеж,
туда, где верность
в то время почиталась вровень
с богами хлеба.
Никто не ждет меня в том граде.
Кто ждал — тот предал.
И я возьму с собой двенадцать
головок лука,
чтоб с головой моей тринадцать
головок было.
Ведь лук —
последнее растенье живой природы
и в эту эру
исторгающее слезы.

И обращусь я к самодержцу:
— Ты в самом деле
сам держишься?
        И сам всё держишь?
— Всё держит стража.
И сам немножечко держусь.
Народ, навроде,
меня поддерживает сам...
        как скажет стража.

И я на площадь положу —
пускай поплачут —
мой лук,
наивные останки живой природы.

В краю,
где столько веков
выковывали бодрость,
снимали голову, как лапоть,
где за слезинку
снимали голову, как лапоть,
где за слезинку
срезали голову, как прыщик, —
рыдала стража!
Народ производил рыданья
поголовно.
Сам самодержец, вождь серьезный,
звезда на зобе,
заместо слизи кусая слезы,
предался злобе.

Но не забыли меня казнить
и не забыли
зарыть двенадцать головок лука
в ближайший омут.

Когда-нибудь, потом, гораздо
позднее, после
взойдет над городом
двенадцать головок лука
и голова моя взойдет
предупрежденьем:
я не последний из казненных,
не последний.

* * *

Но говорят, что город Китеж
никто не видел
Что ж, предположим:
никто не видел.
Предположим...

Gleb Jacovlevich Gorbovsky

It was grey and intensely cold when I first went to see Gorbovsky. He lives in Kupchina, one of the new sections of Leningrad—tall, block-like, identical nine story buildings, exactly similar to the section on the other side of town where Sosnora lives. Gorbovsky lives at the very end of the bus line, remote from all the familiar city landmarks. His is the last apartment building standing on the edge of an open field. Beyond it stretches the infinity of Russia.

He opened the door himself, a gruff, husky, shaggy man. Behind him, in the living room, were three people, a small, dark painter from Moscow who was idly strumming a guitar, another silent, blue-eyed man, also from Moscow, and a blonde girl. They did not move but scrutinized me intently.

The apartment was large but bare; two rooms plus a kitchen and a bathroom. There were two camp beds, one on each side of the living room, one chair, a few books scattered on the window sill, and two or three more on a shelf over one of the camp cots. On the shelf too, were two candy box coloured paintings, one of a Russian church and the other of the head of a woman in surrealist style. A large, old radio stood in a corner. On the opposite wall hung a poster, a huge portrait of the head of Mayakovsky done for exhibit. It was a good painting. Mayakovsky looked like a pop hero of Soviet labour; his strong jaw and burning eyes were as alive as in photographs of him. Gorbovsky said that he had found the poster lying in a gutter on a street in Leningrad. He had rescued it, cleaned the mud off, ironed it, and hung it on his wall.

On the radio there was a bottle of vodka, one glass, and one orange. The glass was passed around to everyone; Gleb ate the orange, spitting out the seeds while he talked. A pile of paintings was stacked in a corner by the door. "They bring them to me," Gleb said and started scattering them helter-skelter on the beds and floor for us to look at. He showed no interest in them himself. His own favourite artist, he said, was Hieronymous Bosch.

Gleb is a bear of a man. Six feet tall, very husky, he has the broad, square body and bright blue eyes of a Russian peasant in a fairy tale. The eyes scrutinize everything, and behind their bright gaze there is intense suspicion. With the suppressed surliness and moodiness of a bear, he waits to see what the stranger brings. He approaches first with caution, even hostility, but once reassured, he becomes expansive and generous as a child. Full of restless energy and raw power, he is—like Russia itself—overwhelmingly larger than life.

That day he was wearing a shaggy, roughly knit, grey-green turtle neck sweater, an old tan jacket, dark grey pants that kept riding up to show heavy navy blue underwear, and rough, thick, black-soled shoes. He has a broad, round face and a shock of soft, brown hair. One thinks immediately of Dylan Thomas—a Russian Dylan Thomas. There is the same carousing character, rough romance, the same brilliance and drama in reading. He dominates a room, everything seems too small for him, the ceilings too low, the chairs too fragile. A force of nature, he booms and thunders in a gruff, growling voice, a speech full of slang and vulgarisms, colloquial but strong. There are few periods to his sentences. He does not like direct questions. He rambles, abruptly shifting subjects as a new thought strikes him. His conversation seesaws between raw jokes and serious, thoughtful analysis of other poets' work. He admires Pushkin—"of course"—and Tsvetayeva and Chorny. He criticizes another poet for being "too European". He gesticulates, waving his broad arms, hunching himself up. Putting a finger to the side of his nose, he tells an anecdote in a confidential tone, then roars with laughter and punctuates the air with his fists. On his square hands are two badly done tattoos, a residue from his boyhood days; on the right hand a rising sun, and on the left an anchor with the initials GG.

Three fat pigeons landed on his window sill. "I feed them only sweets," he said and went off to get some chocolate.

Gleb drank in spurts, but steadily. He toasted, offered the one glass, got another. After an hour or so, a frying pan of eggs and ham appeared, along with a loaf of bread. We all tore off pieces and helped ourselves to whatever pieces of egg and ham we could spear. Between bites, we drank more vodka, and when that ran out, lemonade. Eventually, somebody went out for more vodka.

At first, Gleb was reticent about reading his verses and asked someone else to do it. From the kitchen his wife Svetlana kept insisting sharply, "Read yourself!" He often forgot his own lines, and someone else would take over and recite until he could pick it up again. He recited *Flat Number 6*, his most popular poem and first success, about life in a communal flat in Leningrad. He is a fine actor when he reads. In this poem, he created all the roles, changing voices. His eyes narrowed and widened, his arms flailed, he spat, he shouted, then dropped his voice to a whisper. He became, in turn, a retired colonel, a crochety old lady, then other characters, first melancholy, then wheedling, drunk, gay, philosophical, like a peasant spinning tales through the long winter nights. Later, when he read his shorter poems, he read quietly, meditatively, until, suddenly moved, he exploded again into a shout. We were—as his audiences always are—totally riveted by his performance.

Gorbovsky is perhaps the most Russian of all the Leningrad poets. His strengths and weaknesses are those which Russians consider their own. Perhaps this is why he is so popular and much beloved by his audiences. They say, "That is our Gleb", and flock to hear him whenever he reads. Dozens of songs have been made from his biting, sardonic and funny verses—published and unpublished. He is the rowdy with the heart of gold. He belongs to the city.

Gorbovsky was born in Leningrad on October 4, 1931, and lived on a little street, Malaya Padyezhda, on Vassilevsky Island; the street is famous because Dostoyevsky once lived there. Except for short periods and during the war, Gleb has always lived in Leningrad; his poetry is imbued with his city. He constantly refers to it, to its landmarks and to the countryside around. He is part of it, and it is part of him, inseparably. He writes:

> "I am the city
> One and the same creation
> It is the radiance
> I am the combustion"

His father was a railroad construction engineer and worked all his life on the railroads. When Gleb was a small boy before the war, he lived for periods in Archangel and along the Volga, following his father's work. Later, his father worked on the construction of the White Sea Canal, built by forced labour. Gleb lived in these camps as a boy. Through the siege, when his father had gone to war, he lived in German-occupied territory in the countryside not far from the encircled city. A persistent legend is that he was a pickpocket, stealing ingeniously from the Germans. What certainly is true is that he still remembers a kind of occupation-jargon German with which he still peppers his conversation. During this period when he was still a boy, he began to drink and smoke. The tattoos on his hands are from those days. His friends say, "He was one of the wild boys, with no supervision after the war." Yet he adores his parents and his eyes mist when he talks of his mother.

Gorbovsky had almost no formal schooling, barely finishing the primary grades. At eighteen, he was enrolled in a special trade school for skilled workers and learned cabinet making and how to make mahogany furniture. In 1955, he decided to enroll in the Mining Institute, where he was trained as a working geologist. He has made many geological expeditions, mainly in Siberia, many as far as Kamchatka on the coast of the Northern Pacific. Today, even though he is a member of the Writers' Union, he still goes on geological expeditions every summer. He has been married twice, and from his first marriage has two teenaged children. His first wife was Lydia Gladkaya, also a Leningrad poet who is sometimes published in *Den Poezii*.

In the Mining Institute, Gleb joined one of the poetry circles led by Gleb Semeonov, and it was for this group that Gorbovsky first began to write poetry. The collected poems of the Mining Institute group (which also at that time included Ageev, Kuklin, and Gorodnitsky) were circulated in mimeographed form. In 1957 a public evening of poetry was organized. Called "First Meeting", it was the first occasion when the verses of Gorbovsky, Sosnora, Kushner, and Ufland were read.

Gleb began that evening with a reading of *Flat Number 6*

which, while far from one of his best works, was an instant popular success. It is a poem which, unfortunately, means little to anyone who has not lived in a communal apartment, being constructed of slang and colloquialisms. This poem gave him his first fame and even today Gleb rarely reads in public without being asked to recite it.

Despite his great public popularity, he had trouble having his first book published. He had at that time a "scoundrel fame" for his wild evenings and his run-ins with the militia for rowdiness. He went to an editor with several hundred verses. (Gleb is enormously prolific and almost never goes anywhere without a notebook crammed with poems. He has several such notebooks.) The editor told him that there were not enough verses and to bring more. Gleb brought several hundred more the next day. Confronted with this torrent of words, the editor and his colleagues decided that Gleb had written enough to be published.

In 1960, Gorbovsky's first book, *Poiski Tepla* (Search for Warmth) appeared. He was made a member of the Writers' Union in 1963, on the same day as Victor Sosnora and like him, after the publication of only one book. This was a tribute to Gleb's public popularity, for at the time certain conservative members of the Writers' Union strongly objected to his admission on the grounds that he was a well known hooligan.

His second book, *Spasibo Zemlya*, (Thank you, Earth) was published in 1964, his third, *Kosiye Suchiya* (Crooked Boughs) in 1966. *Tishina* (Stillness) was published in 1968 in an edition of 50,000 copies, every one of which disappeared within a few days. Shortly after its publication, this book was criticised in the newspaper *Sovetskaya Rossiya* as being paranoid, reflecting too much despair and being too preoccupied with pessimistic thoughts. Gleb was quoted out of context from one of his poems as saying, "I am a wild beast." After this, although he was still regularly published in literary journals, he read very little, saying he wanted to be quiet and think.

For the past ten years he has earned his living primarily by writing children's books and verses, for which he is also very well known. In 1971 he wrote a children's play which was performed at the children's theatre in Leningrad.

During the past year and a half, Gorbovsky's boistering personality for which he was so famous has changed a great deal. He has stopped smoking and drinking completely. Now he sips cranberry juice and watches thoughtfully while others grow boisterous. He is mellower, gentler, the gruff voice has lowered. About to turn forty, he looks ten years younger. His bright searching eyes are still the eyes of a merry, generous child, but behind them there is pain. His smile is wry, philosophical. The poetry in his latest book, aptly titled *Novoye Leto* (New Summer) which appeared in the fall of 1971 reflects this new period in his life. He writes:

> To me the summer
> has once more returned!
> How constant the skies . . .
> And from the battered likeness
> sometimes—the eyes still play the fool!
> It is not for me to teach the gloomy, miracles.
> To plunge them into storms of meetings
> and partings.
> We put on happiness
> like a cold,
> and—as quickly recover.

All of Gorbovsky's expansive personal traits carry into his poetry. He embodies in his work many qualities which Russians hold dear, most particularly the quality they call "heart". By this they mean a deep sense of humanity, a fatalistic understanding of the vagaries of life, a profound love of the Russian land and nature—and sentiment. Western taste would sometimes call this sentimentality. Many things concerning the heart and soul can be said in Russian which sound excessive in English.

Russia is a nation with a unique capacity to produce, as if from the land itself, natural, unformed poetic talent. Gorbovsky writes poetry for the same reason a bird sings: it is his nature.

He writes in this spontaneous Russian tradition. He is reminiscent of Yesenin in his perfect feel for the beauties of nature and the Russian countryside. He knows nothing of foreign languages and has no connection or interest in foreign writers. For him, Russia is the world. He has the Russian peasant's melancholy, the same sensitive feeling for the earth, the same suspicious and shrewd instincts about the threatening world outside. Like Yesenin, he seems a country lad caught in the city, a rustic thrown into urban life, confronting the cataclysms of the twentieth century.

Bulat Okudzhava, the famous balladeer poet of Moscow wrote these lines about Gorbovsky in one of his poems:

Why does the poet Gorbovsky hasten to the forest?
To make there, the sketch of his own soul.

It is a surprise to find that this man who could be so rough in person, is always gentle and humble in his poetry: "I am a quiet dwarf living in a tree hollow", "I would like to turn into a fine rain." He compares himself to humble objects, "an old ramshackle tarantass", (a Russian peasant cart) "a grey mouse". In his sense of the greyness of everyday life, his search for communion with nature, his desire to return to a simpler, purer existence, he is particularly contemporary and has links with the philosophy of the flower children in the United States, of whom he knows nothing.

Gorbovsky is a landscape artist. He has a remarkable gift for capturing in a few words the whole atmosphere of a scene. He always draws in a few quick, short strokes, leaving his reader to fill in the rest. For him, the scene is almost always Leningrad; he comes back continually to the city with which his whole life is linked. "I divide the city into kilometres, down to the last street of Leningrad," he writes, or "On the overflowing day when you fell in love in the solemn presence of the Neva."

Vladimir Soloviev, a Soviet critic writing in *Den Poezii*, says, "Nature, for Gorbovsky, is not a temple, not a panacea, not an object of observation, but rather all these things together—a best friend from whom one can learn everything and to whom one can tell everything, the confessor and the confessed."

A part of Gorbovsky's close relationship with the world of nature (which he addressses in the familiar form in Russian) stems from his day to day outdoor life on geological expeditions. But his search for total communion with nature has led him to try to achieve the same communion with men—and here he is often disappointed. Guessing at the possibility of total harmony among people, demanding more than the ordinary person in his relationships, he has failed to reach his own high goals. This non-perfection, non-communion in his own relationships bothers him deeply. This tension in his personality is continually expressed in his work. In his poetry, the prosaic, the public, even the vulgar tongue co-exist with beautiful, lyric language. These prosaicisms at times destroy his verses, or make him appear eclectic or sentimental. He has a tendency to be glib. His faults are extensions of his virtues.

Gorbovsky is at his best in the short form. His most recent poems have become increasingly tight, ever shorter, more ironic and philosophical. In their perfect simplicity they are often reminiscent of haiku. As Soloviev says, "At his best Gorbovsky sees the world with the penetrating precision of a poetic vision which is impeccable, with the exactness of a lyric talent which is immense, and with an extraordinary sensitivity."

SHOUT, GROAN, MEOW

Shout, groan, meow,
Squeal and howl like a saw,
split down the sides
from sound,
But down with silence!
Bears, where are you?
Bend me
into a bow,
into a ring.
You, cracks in granite,
destroy my face!
All roars and squeaks
deprive my soul of sleep . . .
. . . . I want to smash
into spray
like a drunken breaker.

КРИЧАТЬ, СТОНАТЬ, МЯУКАТЬ

Кричать, стонать, мяукать,
визжать и выть пилой,
трещать по швам
от звуков,
но тишину — долой!
Медведи, где вы?
Гните
в дугу меня,
в кольцо.
Вы, трещины в граните,
разрушьте мне лицо!
Все грохоты и писки,
лишайте душу сна...
...Хочу разбиться
в брызги,
как пьяная волна!

I AM A DWARF IN A TREE HOLLOW

I am a quiet dwarf in a tree hollow.
A small nocturnal forester.
I have done no one any harm
But people are displeased with me.
I drink the dew, crack nuts,
And I yawn at the moon.
And yet they say I have committed
Some frightful crime.
Sometimes I sing, my voice no louder
Than the singing of the grass.
Yet often I am threatened by another,
Shouting that I am wrong.
I hide out in my tree hollow;
As to my crime,
No one on earth knows what it is
Neither God nor the devil.

Я ТИХИЙ КАРЛИК ИЗ ДУПЛА

Я тихий карлик из дупла,
лесовичок ночной.
Я никому не сделал зла,
но недовольны мной.

Я пью росу, грызу орех,
зеваю на луну.
И все же очень страшный грех
вменяют мне в вину.

Порой пою, и голос мой
не громче пенья трав.
Но часто мне грозит иной,
кричит, что я неправ!

Скрываюсь я в своем дупле,
и, в чем моя вина,
никто не знает на земле,
ни бог, ни сатана.

I SIT BY THE WINDOW FRAME

I sit by the window frame.
I do not want
to stir.
I was born—
Simply from my mother
But I could have been born
a bird.

Я СИЖУ ЗА ОКОННОЙ РАМОЙ

Я сижу за оконной рамой,
мне не хочется
шевелиться...
Родила меня —
просто мама,
а могла бы родить —
птица.

THE DAY MELTS LIKE SUGAR

The day melts like sugar
in a grey rainsoaked shopping net.
In my heart there is no dread
only blood, coursing . . .
I am again alive!
The insinuating fog discreetly
creeps toward home.
. . . Possible again to dream, to think,
to weigh joys and torments.
The hens toil in the barnyard
A cat, drowsing, tumbles from a doorstep.
Someone mournfully plays
endlessly on an accordion.
How precious to have such moments:
contacts with stillness . . .
How good that for all who wish it,—
there is contemplation of a new night.
And that—like lamps in the sky—
simply,
people may gaze
on the stars!

ДЕНЬ РАСТАЯЛ, СЛОВНО САХАР

День растаял, словно сахар,
в серой сетке дождевой.
В сердце нет ни капли страха, —
только кровь...
Я вновь живой!
Подползает осторожно
к дому вкрадчивый туман.
...Помечтать, подумать можно,
взвесить радость и дурман.
Куры маются в сарае.
В дрёме кот упал с крыльца.
Кто-то жалобно играет
на гармони без конца.
Хорошо, что есть мгновенья:
к тишине прикосновенья...
Что доступно тем, кто хочет, —
созерцанье новой ночи.
Что — как лампы в небе —
просто
можно видеть людям
звёзды!

I AM MINED

I am mined.
A sign
should be hung on my breast.
A tomtit landed on my hat—
Fly away quickly, fool!
A gnat sits on my sleeve.
The little bandit cannot know
what sort of blow threatens him:
the mine will go off,
and he's done for.
A girl comes into sight,
she comes slipping up to me.
Do not come near!
Do not touch!
A splinter will cut you in two.
And all is bliss and silence,
while I live like a stone.
But now spring will come again,
and my body
will be torn to shreds!

J.S.

Я ЗАМИНИРОВАН

Я заминирован.
Табличку
повесить надо на груди.
...На шапку села мне синичка, —
скорее, дура, прочь лети!
На рукаве сидит комар.
Не знает маленький разбойник,
какой грозит ему
удар:
взорвется мина,
и — покойник.
Маячит девушка вдали,
она ко мне вприпрыжку
чешет.
Не подходи!
Не шевели!
Осколком надвое
разрежет.

...И благодать, и тишина,
пока живу
окаменело.
Но вот придет опять весна, —
и разорвется в клочья
тело!

STIR UP, LIKE AN ANT HILL

Stir up, like an ant hill
The whole world of puzzles and problems.
Why does a cardiac need a coffee pot?
When does an executioner execute himself?
To whom is my darling dearest?
To herself, her husband, or me?
And then, try to discover, will you:
Who is to blame that crocodiles walk lying down?
When did all things alive
And dead, arise? and why?
And why are twins born so,
When you and I were born singly?
Who carries burdens like an ant
Without wanting to become master?
Stir it up, poke it,
Sit down on a tree stump—and watch.

J.S.

РАЗВОРОШИТЬ, КАК МУРАВЕЙНИК

Разворошить, как муравейник,
весь мир загадок и задач.
Зачем сердечнику — кофейник?
Когда казнит себя палач?
Кому любимая дороже,
себе ли, мужу или мне?
А крокодилы ходят лежа,
поди узнай — по чьей вине?
Когда возникло все живое
и неживое? Почему?
И почему родится двойня,
а я и ты — по одному?
Кто муравьем таскает тяжесть,
не пожелав владыкой стать?
Разворошить, разбудоражить!
Сесть на пенек и — наблюдать.

THE CHILDREN IN THE COURTYARD

The children in the courtyard play at war
—the last one.
Someone's grandmother in a cap
is slowly nodding off.
The children
blaze away at the sky with their guns
and bomb
from the air.
Their parents
have made many toys
for their children . . .
The courtyard is sprinkled by some machine.
Grownups are playing dominoes.
The children will grow up
and go to the movies in the evenings.
They will have children too,
theirs will be twice as many . . .
. . . But the children of the grandmother in the cap
are all back there . . .
In the last war.

J.S.

НА ДВОРЕ ИГРАЮТ ДЕТИ —

На дворе играют дети —
в ту,
прошедшую войну...
Чью-то бабушку в берете
клонит медленно ко сну...
Дети
в небо бьют из пушек,
дети
с воздуха
бомбят...
Много сделали игрушек
папы-мамы
для ребят...
Поливает двор
машина.
Дяди бьются
в домино...

Дети станут все
большими,
сходят вечером
в кино...
У детей — родятся дети,
будет больше их
вдвойне.
...А у бабушки в берете
дети — там...
На той войне...

FORTY YEARS HE PLOUGHED
AND SOWED

Forty years he ploughed and sowed,
and now tired
has come to rest.
Flat on Mother Russia,
stretching out the sticks of his legs.
His beard thrust up to heaven,
ruffled,
like grass.
He was never in Paris,
or even in the city of Moscow.
Fists,
like stones,
thrown out by his side.
We will all lie down as old men,
only to lie like this
is not for us!
The wind plucks at his shirt,
or is the blood rebelling in him?
Has he died, the old fellow
or is he drowned in sleep?
The evening plunges him
into its chill,
as into the depths of the ages.
On his nose
a cricket
sat awhile
and then made off.

СОРОК ЛЕТ ПАХАЛ И СЕЯЛ,

Сорок лет пахал и сеял,
а сейчас устал, прилег.
Лег на матушку Расею,
протянул жердины ног.
Борода взметнулась к небу,
закачалась, как трава...
А ведь он в Париже не был,
не был в городе Москва.
Кулаки,
как будто камни,
разбросал по сторонам.
Все мы ляжем
стариками,
только так лежать
не нам.
Ветер рвет его рубашку,
или кровь играет
в нем?
То ли умер старикашка,
то ли спит
мертвецким сном.
Окунает деда вечер
в холодок,
как в глубь веков.
...На носу его
кузнечик
посидел
и был таков.

A WOMAN BIDS GOODBYE TO A HUSBAND

A woman bids goodbye to a husband
She goes, distracted, through puddles
Shivers in her coat—tatters
and sick at heart she is, miserable and cold.

The man already in the depths of his compartment
Had sliced his sausage and bacon,
poured half a glass
drunk it, impassive as an idol.

And the woman trudges homeward
to no one, to hunger and emptiness . . .
While her husband rolls up his napkin
and calmly appraises his pretty neighbour.

ПРОЩАЕТСЯ ЖЕНЩИНА С МУЖЕМ

Прощается женщина с мужем.
Идет, как по небу, по лужам.
Трепещет пальто ее — тряпка,
и скверно ей, верно, и зябко.

Мужчина ж в пучине вагона
нарезал колбас и бекона,
налил половину стакана
и выпил с лицом истукана.

А женщина тащится к дому —
к немому, глухому, пустому...

А муж ее, скомкав салфетку,
спокойно глядит на соседку.

GREEN TIE

I'll buy myself a tie
green as the grass.
I'll sport it on the boulevard—
a real boulevard poet.

My wart,
brown coloured
underneath the bulging cheekbone
Will be in style, and prized accordingly.

Old maids will mutter
"He drinks cocoa in the morning
and vodka over lunch . . ."
Discussing me as if
I were a strange object,
mistakingly reducing
the number of my years.
For them it will be fun
to observe me in this role,
painful for my friends,
Should I have any left.

I'll buy myself a tie
green, as the fields . . .
May he be cruelly cursed—
this clever and future I!

J.S.

ЗЕЛЕНЫЙ ГАЛСТУК

Я куплю себе галстук
зеленый, как травка.
Щегольну по бульвару —
бульварный поэт...
Будет ценной и модной
моя бородавка
под округлой скулою —
коричневый цвет...
Будут старые девы бубнить о поэте:
— Утром пьет он какао...
— Водку пьет он в обед... —
Рассуждая порой обо мне,
как о странном предмете,
будут мне убавлять по ошибке
количество лет.
Будет весело тем
наблюдать меня в этакой роли,
будет больно друзьям...
Если будут друзья.

Я куплю себе галстук,
зеленый, как поле...
Будь он проклят —
разумный и будущий Я!

In the family there is trouble.
The reason—jealousy.
He paces red-faced
over the floorboards,
like a tramway on its rails,
back and forth,
from end to end.
She looks out the window
over the rooftops,
where a crowd of antennae are gathered.
And the sun sinks ever lower
behind the bricks,
behind the backs of walls.
The son is entangled in arithmetic,
ink covered from head to foot.
Everything correct,
it seemed.
There had been a family.
And now—alas . . .
He looks for his hat.
His suitcase trembles slightly in his hand.
He will prove to them!
He will show them . . .
And a vein dances
on his temple.
But having tired,
having foamed a little,
he will steal into the bath,
take a shower
and at the same tempo,
gait slowing,
he will lie down to sleep.
He is a man.
He is a husband.

В СЕМЬЕ СКАНДАЛ

В семье скандал.
Причина — ревность.
Он ходит красный,
как трамвай,
по доскам пола,
как по рельсам,
туда-сюда,
из края в край.
Она глядит в окно
на крыши,
где собралась
толпа антенн.
А солнце падает все ниже
за кирпичи,
за спины стен.
Сын арифметикой опутан
в чернилах с ног до головы.
Все было правильно
как будто.
Была семья.
И вот — увы...
Он ищет шляпу.
Саквояжик
слегка дрожит в его руке.
Он им докажет!
Он покажет...
И пляшет жилка
на виске...
Но приустав,
слюной побрызгав,
залезет в ванну,
примет душ
и в том же темпе,
с той же рысью
заляжет спать.
Мужчина.
Муж.

REQUEST

When I shall grow too old for songs
and for you,
and it will come;
When mould grows on my temples,
and the voice grows weak and complaining,
Then do not lead me to the almshouse:
Lead me, as in a fairy tale,—
to the forest.
There it will be morning,
There will be fir trees,
And something will anoint me
from the sky. . . .

ПРОСЬБА

Когда я буду стар для песен
и для тебя,
а это будет;
когда виски покроет плесень,
а голос станет хил и нуден,
тогда не нужно в богадельню:
свези меня, как в сказке, —
в лес.
То будет утро,
будет ельник,
и что-то будет лить
с небес...

I LIVE IN A LITTLE HOUSE IN THE FOREST

I live in a little house in the forest,
Winter is all about me.
My dwelling has one window,
and a host
of cracks and holes.
My head sneezes
at a hundred and more
problems.
I eat
dried fish
and split firewood.
I have sunk
in this sleepy round of life
up to my head.
. . . Only on my candle
sleeplessly
plays
a flame. . . .

J.S.

ЖИВУ Я В ДОМИКЕ ЛЕСНОМ

Живу я в домике лесном.
Вокруг меня — зима.
Моё жильё
с одним окном.
Щелей и дырок —
тьма.
На сто и более
проблем
чихает голова...
Я рыбку вяленую
ем,
колю свои дрова.
Я погружён в дремучий быт
от головы до ног...
...Лишь на свече моей не спит,
резвится
огонёк...

Night. A path.
The moon shines full.
Branches brush the face.
The forest creatures have retired.
The trembling of the grass has ceased.
In the stream, fishlings
have closed their glassy eyes.
At this hour,
they don't give a damn
for me—
Tsar of nature.
In my boot an old bunion
is aching miserably . . .
. . . Who am I to bear the world's burdens?
to be the boss,
the navel of the earth,
let alone, the salt . . .
Through rocks and bracken
I silently pick my way,
like an old ramshackle tarantass
over the potholes of being.

НОЧЬ. ТРОПА

Ночь. Тропа.
Луна в разгаре.
Ветки шарят по лицу.
Улеглись лесные твари,
травы сбросили
трясцу.
В речке будущие шпроты
притушили рыбий глаз.
На меня,
царя природы,
наплевать им в этот час.
В сапоге скулит печально,
ноет
старая мозоль.
Никакой я
не начальник,
пуп земли,
а также — соль...
Меж камней
и меж орясин
пробираюсь молча я,
словно старый
тарантасик
на ухабах бытия.

THERE IS A MAN BEHIND ME

There is a man behind me.
He has been walking at my back for a long time.
I change my routes,
I wander round in all directions,
Charge into shops and public baths,
And dive, a grey mouse, into the subway.
But now, three of them
trudge behind me.
I purchase a newspaper at the kiosk.
I do not smoke, but chew my cigarette.
I run from yesterday into tomorrow,
But a whole hundred are already after me.
Trying to lose them,
I decide to go to the beach . . .
And strip.
I cover myself with the newspaper . . .
And—God!—what do you think?
There are so many of them
That, bending my submissive shoulders
I quietly walk forward to meet them.

J.S.

ЧЕЛОВЕК ЗА МОЕЮ СПИНОЮ

Человек за моею спиною.
Он идет уже долго за мною.
Я меняю маршруты,
плутаю,
в магазины и в бани
влетаю;
серой мышью ныряю
в метро я,
а за мной уже топают
трое.
Покупаю в киоске газету,
не курю, а жую сигарету,
из вчера выбегаю в сегодня,
а за мной уже — целая сотня.
Я стараюсь от них отвертеться.
Я решаю на пляже
раздеться.
Накрываюсь газетой...
И что же?
Их такое количество — боже! —
что, сутуля покорные плечи,
я тихонько иду им
навстречу.

THE CALENDAR LIES

The calendar lies,
having scattered its dates;
like regiments,
the months close in.
. . . My days like soldiers
march past life,
which waves at them from doorsteps.
Never,
neither in daylight, nor at night,
will I reveal the secret of my living.
It may be I am lonelier than a dog,
drifting about the town without pilot lights
among friends and telephone booths,
with a blank smile across my face . . .
I shall return,
I shall often return.
There is no point, old woman,
in waving from the doorstep!
The calendar, a catalogue of sighs and victories,
and departures at night . . .
Outside the windows, our era rattles by,
and it is not I,
but it,
that calls for help.

J.S.

КАЛЕНДАРЬ ЛЕЖИТ

Календарь лежит,
рассыпав даты;
как полки́,
сомкнулись месяца.
...Дни мои,
идущие солдаты
мимо жизни,
машущей с крыльца.
Никогда,
ни белым днем, ни ночью,
не открою тайну,
чем живу.
Может, я собаки одиноче,
без огней по городу плыву
меж друзей и телефонных будок,
с белою улыбкой на лице...

Я вернусь,
я возвращаться буду,
зря ты, тетка,
машешь на крыльце!
Календарь — таблица наших вздохов,
и побед,
и уезжаний в ночь...

Тарахтит за окнами эпоха,
и не мне,
а нужно — ей
помочь.

TOWARDS AUTUMN

Snow falls on the yellow leaves.
In the sky branches creak.
Along the road I went,
Along the road to her . . .
Slowly, as a tree,
quietly, as an old man.
Two steps away
a startled swallow appeared.
Mingled with leaves
snow
and all is dense.
. . . I went, as to a refuge,
towards my autumn.

К ОСЕНИ

Снег — на листья желтые.
В небе — крик ветвей.
По дороге шел я,
по дороге к ней...
Медленный, как дерево,
тихий, как старик.
В двух шагах растерянный
воробей возник.
Перемешан с листьями
снег
и всё — плотней.
...Шел я, словно к пристани,
к осени моей.

IT'S NOT BY CHANCE I WAS BORN IN OCTOBER

It's not by chance I was born in October,
in such an amazing time.
. . . It was pouring rain
that seemed heavier in front of the street light,
etched in the darkness of the street.
Women gave birth,
and in the howling of autumn
and the Body—
I was born . . .
and at once began to run
from the darkness into the light,
towards the new limit.

And now again—
October is over me.
Trees—
already half asleep and clinging.
And a woman,
swollen with spring,—
is just ahead of me . . .
and I—wear a rain drenched cap.

НЕДАРОМ Я РОДИЛСЯ В ОКТЯБРЕ

Недаром я родился в октябре,
в такое удивительное время.
...Лил дождь
и был крупней при фонаре,
что в уличную вписывался темень.
Беременные ехали рожать,
И в завываньи осени
и Тела —
родился я...
И сразу же — бежать
из тьмы на свет,
до нового предела.

И вот опять —
октябрь надо мной.
Деревья —
так же заспанны и цепки.
И женщина,
набухшая весной, —
чуть впереди...
И я — в промокшей кепке.

IN THE GARDEN THE FLOWERS ARE HALF-WITHERED

The flowers in the garden are half withered,
In a short while they will be dead.
The sun between the clouds
No longer warms my head.
I fear the shades of autumn,
When the snow's suddenly upon us . . .
I am afraid,
like every mean and dark
And lonely man.

J.S.

В САДУ ЦВЕТЫ ПОЛУЗАВЯЛИ

В саду цветы полузавяли,
еще немного и — мертвы.
Меж туч светило —
как в провале,
моей не греет головы.
Боюсь осенних помрачений,
когда вот-вот
и грянет снег...
Боюсь,
как всякий злой, вечерний
и одинокий человек.

JUST ONE MORE TIME

Just one more time
to fall in love to suffocation
to the explosion of the heart.
And then to grow numb.
Soul drained,
like a dried up puddle.
No more taste
for exquisite fare:
for grouse,
or the songs of minstrels. . . .
Just one more time
to feel the breathtaking flight of wings
so that from ecstasy
plumage singed,
the old skin sheds.
But if not . . .
Then on with your galoshes,
to find a wet bench
in the park . . . .
With what dream,
with what sweet lie
have the years enticed away
my youth?

ЕЩЕ БЫ РАЗ

Еще бы раз
влюбиться до удушья,
до взрыва сердца.
И окостенеть.
Душа пуста,
как высохшая лужа.
Не лезет в рот
изысканная снедь:
ни рябчики,
ни пенье менестрелей...
Еще бы раз —
щемящий лет крыла.
Чтоб от восторга
перья обгорели,
чтоб с тела кожа старая
сползла.
А если нет...
Тогда надеть галоши,
найти в саду
холодную скамью...
Какой мечтой,
какою сладкой ложью
сманили годы
молодость мою?

Try
to describe weariness,
when the future holds
so few good words,
and the terrible words,
are beyond counting!
I had a beloved . . .
who like the morning
bestowed a wise light.
But she has tired,
a frail object
who has drifted into the past.
One cannot recapture,
either at a resort,
nor in long unconscious slumber,
what has been lost, corrupted,
or consumed in flame.
Still,
I am always drawn to the forest.
To hide myself away in the lonely places.
One last time.
Moorings for mortals
are much the same,
only their hour of death varies.
I have fingered volcanoes,
touched the sea,
caressed forests and cities.
Yet the road is not overgrown with anguish,
not blocked forever.

ПОПРОБУЙ

Попробуй
опиши усталость,
когда осталось впереди
хороших слов
такая малость,
а страшных слов
поди сочти!
Была любимая...
Что утро
она дарила мудрый свет.
Но и она устала —
утлый,
уплывший в прошлое
предмет.
Не наверстать
ни на курорте,
ни в долгом обморочном сне,
что потерял, или испортил,
или изжарил на огне.
Меня все тянет в лес,
однако.
Забиться в глушь.
Последний раз.
Причал у смертных
одинаков,
не одинаков смертный час.
Вулканы щупал,
море трогал,
ласкал леса и города.
Не заросла тоской дорога,
не оборвалась навсегда.
Еще иду.

I still do walk.
Past me hurtle
posts, iron bridges.
But there is a weariness. . . .
And from my beloved there remains a trace,
as from a star.

И мчатся мимо
столбы, железные мосты.
Но вот усталость...
От любимой
остался след,
как от звезды.

IN THE NIGHT

To A. Kushner

In the night the joints of the sick,
cold,
dacha creak.
And I hear how wearily
canters the tardy horseman.
Every day. Without fail.
Who is he?
Ghost—or village doctor?
Head of the whole universe
or someone
of lesser importance?
Farmer? Kolkhoz watchman?
During the summer we have grown close.
Soon it will be evening.
Which means that soon
people will crawl into their television sets.
Someone will open a book
Someone will caress his love.
Wind, hoarse from howling.
Ragged rain,
almost a blizzard.
Now the night hides the trees.
But where is the horseman?
I wonder why he gallops no longer.
why his hooves have grown silent?
I have not slept for two nights running.
Something has happened in nature.
It has grown foul, grown terrifying
in our dacha's orchard.
Soon, probably, the sleepy snow
will drift around the house.
Isn't it time, children, to go to the city?
So then, gather up your toys.

ПО НОЧАМ ХРУСТЯТ СУСТАВЫ

А. Кушнеру

По ночам хрустят суставы
у больной,
холодной дачи.
И я слышу,
как устало
запоздалый всадник скачет.
Ежедневно. Неизменно.
Кто он?
Призрак или — фельдшер?
Председатель всей вселенной
или кто-нибудь
помельче?
Агроном? Колхозный сторож?
Мне он стал за лето близок.
Скоро вечер.
Значит, скоро
люди влезут в телевизор.
Кто-нибудь разломит книгу,
кто-нибудь погладит друга.
Ветер давится от крика.
Дождь лохматый,
точно вьюга.
Вот и ночь деревья прячет.
Где же всадник?
Любопытно,
почему же он не скачет,
почему молчат копыта?
Я не сплю вторые сутки.
Что-то там стряслось в природе.
Стало скверно. Стало жутко
В нашем дачном огороде.
Неплывет, наверно, скоро
сонный снег вокруг избушки...
Не пора ли, дети, в город?
Собирайте-ка игрушки.

Alexander Semyonovich Kushner

Alexander Kushner was born in Leningrad on September 14, 1936 the only son of a Lieutenant Colonel of the Army Engineers. His mother worked as an office manager. His is a respected family; his father's uncle was Boris Kushner, minor poet, Futurist writer, a friend of Mayakovsky and the Futurist group in Moscow.

Young Alexander Kushner had a gentle and proper upbringing. During the Blockade years, he was evacuated and spent the war years in the south of Russia. He had full academic education: following his Baccalaureat, he completed the five-year programme at Leningrad's Herzen Pedagogical Institute, the most prestigious institute for the training of teachers in the Soviet Union. This school has twelve faculties, 30,000 resident students, and many more corresponding students who come from all over Russia to Leningrad to take their final exams. The Institute, whose professors are among the most distinguished in Leningrad, sends its graduates as teachers throughout the USSR. In the past, there were a number of foreign language schools in Leningrad, but Herzen is now the city's major centre for the study of English, French, and German.

Kushner reads and understands French, a rarer accomplishment than in the past, since English has replaced French as the most common second language. Over the past ten years he has been a teacher of Russian literature from the eighteenth century to Yevtushenko and Voznesensky. In addition, he taught Russian language to young workers in the Vyborgsky section of Leningrad. Today he works only on his poetry translations and criticism.

He is perhaps the most officially respected and established poet of his generation in Leningrad. Very much in the Petersburg classical tradition of Pushkin, Blok, and Akhmatova, his verses are philosophical, disciplined, and transparently clear in style. A gentle, scholarly man, he is typical of the writing Russian poet, rather than the declaiming or singing poet. His first book, *Pervye Vpechatlenia* (First Impressions), was published in 1962, his second,

Nochnoy Dozor (Night Watch), in 1966, and his third, *Primyety* (Signs), in the summer of 1969. He was made a member of the Writers' Union in 1966 after the publication of his second book. In addition, he publishes regularly in all the literary journals of Leningrad. In 1968 he served on the editorial board of *Den Poezii*. A new book of his poems is in preparation, but will not be published for two or three years.

Kushner says, "The words of Kuzmin are eternal" and he considers this poet, along with Akhmatova and Baratynsky, to be the greatest influences on his own work. He greatly admires Mandelstam. Although he is quite individual in his poetic form, his artistic interests place him close to Brodsky, Rein and Naiman. All these poets are ethnically Jewish (although not practising Jews), intellectual, cultured, well-read, and tend to be regarded by other poets as "different" and "less Russian".

In his manner of life, Kushner is the opposite of Gorbovsky. Physically, he is small and very quiet. He has a mass of black hair, always carefully combed, very black eyes, velvet and sad, always covered by heavy glasses. He wears a conservative dark suit, a white shirt, a dark tie, conservative coat and gloves. He could easily be a serious young professor in any large European university. He loves the music of Bach and Mozart, he is interested in the painting of Bakst and Golovin. Among foreign writers, he especially admires Camus and Proust, and indeed could be a Proust character himself. He is delicately courteous and polite, like the hero of a nineteenth-century Russian novel.

Kushner is so timid and sensitive that he cannot bear to offend or publicly contradict any other poet except in the mildest way, even when his own arguments are better considered, which they often are. And although he does not agree with others most of the time, and is often artistically disturbed by experimentation, his objections are always phrased in the gentlest, most polite manner. He is fair. His criticism is never destructive. Therefore, he suffers from the free-wheeling, loud poetical arguments which to some other poets are essential sustenance. One evening I was with Kushner when several other young poets were reciting, arguing, and drinking. As the evening wore on, after they had dissected his work, Kushner was pushed to recite. His hands grew cold; he is painfully shy about reading his verses and seldom does so in public. Pushed and bullied, close to panic, he finally began to recite in a thin, breathless, high pitched, almost inaudible voice, pleadingly looking for strength now to the ceiling, then to the floor, never at his audience. His verses are musical, harmonious and delicate in Russian. His themes are classical ones: life, death, liberty, eternity, the nature of the soul. He looks to the sky and to nature for serenity and never ceases questioning the reasons for human existence.

After he had read, I thanked him and told him I would like to see and talk to him in a quieter moment. He seemed relieved and happy and said, Yes, Yes, he would like me to come to his home and to meet his wife. Earlier, he had told me with great pride about her and her accomplishments in French.

We met one freezing, grey, windy morning. He was dressed as usual in a dark, conservative suit, a small, grey astrakhan hat and black gloves. His wife, Tanya, was with him. She is a tall, red-headed, green-eyed, gracious woman. She wore a fine warm coat with a fur collar. We huddled together arm in arm against the cold wind and walked to a taxi stop. It was a long ride through a section of Leningrad unknown to me, devastated by the war and rebuilt in solid Stalinesque architecture. On every building were giant red banners proclaiming "Glory to the Communist Party", "Glory to Soviet Construction" and "Lenin lives". It looked like Moscow, not Leningrad. We finally came to their street, a block reminiscent of New York's West Side, with large, stolid apartment buildings.

Their apartment is large and old-fashioned with a comfortable, well-lived-in look. As I walked into the vestibule, I saw a large refrigerator at the end of the long wall. By the door was a full-length mirror and many wooden pegs for hanging coats.

I was taken into Kushner's study, a small, immaculately organized room. There was a large, solid desk, perfectly clean except for pencils and pens arranged in a row. One entire wall was covered with large glassed-in bookshelves. There was a warm, old-fashioned couch and two chairs. It was very much a professor's study. On the wall were two Goncharova etchings given to him by Lydia Ginzburg. (In his latest volume he dedicates two poems to her.)

Tanya is a teacher of French literature in the secondary schools. She speaks French slightly better than Sasha and admires Camus and Proust as much as he. On their shelves were Balzac, Stendhal and many other French classics. All the editions of *Den Poezii* and other Russian literary magazines were neatly lined up, followed by a row of dictionaries.

Before a TV set in one of the bedrooms, Sasha's father was watching a hockey match, with his grandson. The boy was brought in to greet me. Eugene is a husky child, now ten, who looks much like his mother. Tanya asked if I was hungry and bustled out into the kitchen to return with a bottle of champagne and some oranges. (It was 11 a.m.) We drank the champagne, toasting poetry, and then she went back to the kitchen to bring sausages, cheese, eggs, black bread and butter, and a large can of mango juice from India. We talked quietly until early afternoon. Sasha insisted on accompanying me personally by taxi the long distance back to the centre of the city. When we parted, he bowed and thanked me and then set off to take the Metro home.

Kushner is often discussed by his fellow Leningrad poets. Since breaking old forms and attempting new structures and new ideas is so important to so many of them, they sometimes tend to scorn his modesty of expression and lack of flamboyance. This opinion is by no means unanimous. One talented younger poet declared that Kushner (along with Brodsky) was "one of the two brilliant lights of our poetry". In the harmony and calm of his work, he is following in the finest artistic traditions of Petersburg. The Italian critic Giovanni Buttafava, writing in *Poesia Russa Contemporanea*, says, "If I were to have to give a single name among all the young Soviet poets which I believed would last, I would say 'Kushner'. His poetry is indissolubly linked with the city and the music of Leningrad, a tenuous yet resistant survival of the melody of Petrograd, of the might of the city of Peter." Kushner himself says simply, "The city makes the soul", and believes that the sobriety and harmony of the architecture have had a great influence on his work. Buttafava continues: "In Kushner are concentrated in a crystalline form most of the secrets of the literary tradition which immediately preceded the revolution. In his limpid irony, one discovers the Alexandrine verses, the limpid clarity of Kuzmin; in the essential modesty of his immediate confessions reverberates a little of the acmeism of Akhmatova."

Perhaps most important, Kushner realizes, as Blok did, the intellectual tension between the European concepts and the Russian-Asiatic concepts, and he uniquely fuses the ideas of both. He says, "Leningrad is Europe," yet he is a Russian intellectual and could not be separated from his heritage.

Despite his critics, Kushner is far more than a mere academic imitating a long-ago culture and verse. He has a subtle and exact vision of everyday life. Objects and figures are observed so intensely that he seems to freeze them in space. The houses and scenes of the eternal Leningrad are delicately and precisely etched in time and space.

It is difficult to translate the classical forms and sounds of Kushner. Clear and harmonic in Russian, his carefully thought out verses have difficulty surviving the transition into another language. Yet it is essential to try to read and understand him. For, as Buttafava says, "In the final analysis, the poetry of Kushner which gives the impression of subjectivity and contemplation, perhaps finally says more, in a humble and restrained manner, about the spiritual condition of the young Soviet intellectual than many of those who speak more flamboyantly."

The thoughts and images in poetry are just possible to translate. What is *not*—or too often not—is the particular musicality in which those thoughts and images are couched. Yet it is through this musicality precisely that they cast their spell and hit below the merely conscious mind.

My chief problem in trying to render the poems of Kushner, Kuzminsky, and Sosnora faithfully has been how to re-orchestrate in terms of our own verbal music the tones and rhythms in which the magic of the original was locked. For which reason, over and above what I may have lost in the transposition, even more will escape if these poems are not read aloud, or at least with the mind's ear: which, whatever the dictates of sense, must never be cheated of the sonic value of a line.

P.R.

DEEP AT THE CORE OF THE STILLEST
DEPTHS

Deep at the core of the stillest depths,
Scarcely to be noticed, Death,
Like a grain on the floor of the deep, reflects
A motley glimmer of stippled tints.
Into each wood and field and fresh
Garden creeps a venom more deadly
Than choking grass and virulent tare:
Searing the heart with a covert fire.

As if someone behind a hedge,
Behind a buffet, behind a shed,
Held a ring above the wine:
A secret with a monogram.
Oh how deadly black his spine!
And how his ring glints in the sun!
But without this grain the wine
Has no taste, is not to drain.

P.R.

НО И В САМОМ ЛЕГКОМ ДНЕ

Но и в самом легком дне,
Самом тихом, незаметном,
Смерть, как зернышко на дне,
Светит блеском разноцветным.
В рощу, в поле, в свежий сад,
Злей хвоща и молочая,
Проникает острый яд,
Сердце тайно обжигая.

Словно кто-то за кустом,
За сараем, за буфетом
Держит перстень над вином
С монограммой и секретом.
Как черна его спина!
Как блестит на перстне солнце!
Но без этого зерна
Вкус не тот, вино не пьется.

A STAR BURNS ABOVE THE TREE TOPS

A star above the tree tops
Just short of where it shoots

Cremates itself. The gusts
Are not enough to blast
The pines into the screes

Tempests lash the trees:
Their splendour their demise.

But who adjusts the world
To let the fledgling bird
Sleep inside its nest?

P.R.

ЗВЕЗДА НАД КРОНАМИ ДЕРЕВ

Звезда над кронами дерев
Сгорит, чуть-чуть не долетев.

И ветер дует... Но не так,
Чтоб ели рухнули в овраг.

И ливень хлещет по лесам,
Но, просветлев, стихает сам.

Кто, кто так держит мир в узде,
Что может птенчик спать в гнезде?

Compared with signs of winter
—October or November:
Plain as an infant's writing
Or frost at dawn—the signals

Of your immortal spirit
Are hardly to be sighted.
For whom are the fields for instance
So fine, the woods, the sandpit?

Down a ravine I sidled,
Deep, and not to fall.
The lilac darkness reeled there
And sand rose in a wall:

Red and yellow, violet,
And dazzling white as well.
"Ready?" I whispered. "No, no!"
And dared not look back still.

Such silence I'm not ready
To live, but live the trace
Of life and not the lovely
Sky clouds but their shades.

Nor ready to fly in rings in
This nitrogen of air,
Or scatter snowwhite eider
As a fragment of the heights.

So, give me power to soar:
Lighten me with words.
Take pity, I can still
Not find such radiance small.

P.R.

ПО СРАВНЕНЬЮ С ПРИМЕТАМИ ЗИМ

По сравненью с приметами зим
Где-нибудь в октябре, ноябре,
Что заметны, как детский нажим
На письме, как мороз на заре,

Вы, приметы бессмертья души,
Еле-еле видны. Например,
Для кого так поля хороши,
И леса, и песчаный карьер?

Я спустился в глубокий овраг,
Чтоб не грохнуться — наискосок,
Там клубился сиреневый мрак
И стеной поднимался песок.

Был он красен, и желт, и лилов,
А еще — ослепительно бел.
«Ты готов?» Я шепнул: «Не готов».
И назад оглянуться не смел.

Не готов я к такой тишине!
Не к живым, а к следам от живых!
Не к родным облакам в вышине,
А к теням мимолетным от них!

Не готов я по кругу летать,
В этот воздух входить, как азот,
Белоснежные перья ронять,
Составная частичка высот.

Дай мне силы подняться наверх,
Разговором меня развлеки,
Пощади. Я еще не из тех,
Для кого этот блеск — пустяки.

ALPHABETS

In Latin characters we see
The hills of Rome and vividly
The waves of the Mediterranean:
Foam, the play of fishscales, rings,
Of sheep-bells with the flocks all roaming;
Wine sucked from a shepherd's skin.

But the alphabet of Georgia
Is china shattered by a spear
Or fallen simply off its ledge,
And in the tremulous morning mist,
Ilya, Paolo, Titsian★ must
Gather the fragments' rounded edge.

Then in the Russian "zhe" and "sha"
Lives some flood of spirit's roar,
Turmoil, tempests, froth and forces;
Bantering coachman, tipsy, brash,
In kaftan, ruddy-jowled, and sash,
With hand on hips, who drives his horses.

And here we have Teutonic print:
Letters hard to make distinct—
Like the roofs of Marburg, thick
With lines and contours of gothic.
Cries and footfalls in the night.
Do not wake them! Quiet! Quiet!

Hebrew script flies in the air
Whither? It cannot tell where.
Notations written like a tune.
Quickly take your violin
And press the linen to your chin.
But do not cry, go on playing
Hush, yes, hush! there . . . there

P.R.

★ Three Georgian poets.

БУКВЫ

В латинском шрифте, видим мы,
Сказались римские холмы
И средиземных волн барашки,
Игра чешуек и колец,
Как бы ползут стада овец,
Пастух вино сосет из фляжки.

Зато грузинский алфавит
На черепки мечом разбит
Иль сам упал с высокой полки.
Чуть дрогнет утренний туман —
Илья, Паоло, Тициан
Сбирают круглые осколки.

А в русских буквах «же» и «ша»
Живет размашисто душа,
Метет метель, шумя и пенясь.
В кафтане бойкий ямщичок,
Удал, хмелен и краснощек,
Лошадкой правит, подбоченясь.

А вот немецкая печать,
Так трудно буквы различать,
Как будто марбургские крыши,
Густая готика строки.
Ночные окрики, шаги.
Не разбудить бы! Тише! тише!

Летит еврейское письмо.
Куда? — Не ведает само,
Слова написаны, как ноты.
Скорее скрипочку хватай,
К щеке платочек прижимай,
Не плачь, играй... Ну что ты? Что ты?

THE CENTURY I SEE IS CLEAR

The century I see is clear: the 12th
An ocean or three, some rivers and if
You cried here, there you were heard.
So that a swallow outsailing a ship
Could carry a hair, a single strand,
In its bill to Cornwall from Ireland.

Ah, what a century now, what murk!
Where is the letter? No letter appears
Vainly the waves murmur and break,
Is the romance of Europe erased?
Cancelled with Tristan under the sod?
Are there no swallows? No more, my dear?

P.R.

ЧЕТКО ВИЖУ ДВЕНАДЦАТЫЙ ВЕК

Четко вижу двенадцатый век.
Два-три моря да несколько рек.
Крикнешь здесь — там услышат твой голос.
Так что ласточки в клюве могли
Занести, обогнав корабли,
В Корнуэльс из Ирландии волос.

А сейчас что за век, что за тьма!
Где письмо? Не дождаться письма.
Даром волны шумят, набегая.
Иль и впрямь европейский роман
Отменен, похоронен Тристан?
Или ласточек нет, дорогая?

SPRING

The water is stiff in the garden still
And ungloved fingers freeze; the air
  Translucent, fresh and sweet,
  And blue-black everywhere.

Clouds sail by with little shape,
Unmodelled by the weather still:
Like some faintly silvered freaks
  Swimming in space.

Along the windows of the Winter Palace
—Sometimes violet, sometimes blue—
Black cuneiforms of shadows flying:
Are they swifts or are they starling?

  Or does some connoisseur
Of ancient humpbacked furniture
  Return like a furtive bird
  And from his sepulchre
  A chill whiff of air?

P.R.

ВЕСНА

В саду еще стоит вода,
И зябнут руки без перчаток.
Прозрачный воздух свеж и сладок,
И синь везде и чернота.

Еще лепные облака
Выходят плохо у погоды.
Плывут какие-то уроды,
Посеребренные слегка.

Вдоль стекол Зимнего дворца,
То фиолетовых, то синих,
Мелькает тень на черных клиньях
Не то стрижа, не то скворца.

Не то какой-нибудь знаток
Старинной мебели горбатой
Вернулся птичкой вороватой,
А с ним — загробный холодок.

WHEN IN THE PAVLOVSK PALACE

When in the Pavlovsk Palace
You probed for yourself in a mirror:
Rococo, luxurious, royal,
Decadent . . . all of a sudden
As in a clouded lake
Or in a midnight pond
Somewhere a ripple stirred
And at the end of the Hall
A Fury appeared with a bloated
Face in a ruffled cap.
Soon, from the depths it cleared.
And not without some pain
You floated to the top—
Half bubbling and with sand.
But life for us for a while
Seemed shadowy and fragile.

P.R.

КОГДА ТЫ В ПАВЛОВСКОМ ДВОРЦЕ

Когда ты в Павловском дворце
Искала в зеркале барочном,
Роскошном, царственном, порочном,
Себя — как в тусклом озерце
Иль где-нибудь в пруде полночном, —
Рябь набегала, и в конце
Той залы нам с лицом отечным
Являлась фурия в чепце.
Потом зеркальная вода
Светлела. В ней не без труда
Всплывала ты, с песком проточным
И пузырьками пополам.
Но долго жизнь казалась нам
Туманным делом и непрочным!

THE OLD MAN

What is so still
As an old man staring
At a bird through his final
Hospital window?

. . . Seeing the bushes
Against a kiosk,
Wearing the hospital
Striped pyjamas.

Was he a clerk?
A builder or what?
Whatever, already
He has forgot.

A domino fan?
Stereo tinker?
This window the last
Toy he has got.

P.R.

СТАРИК

Кто тише старика,
Попавшего в больницу,
В окно издалека
Глядящего на птицу?

Кусты ему видны,
Прижатые к киоску.
Висят на нем штаны
Больничные в полоску.

Бухгалтером он был
Иль стекла мазал мелом?
Уж он и сам забыл,
Каким был занят делом.

Сражался в домино
Иль мастерил динамик?
Теперь ему одно
Окно, как в детстве пряник.

HE DANCES WHO DOES NOT DANCE

He dances who does not dance,
Clinking his knife against his glass.
He prances who does not prance,
Bucking and crying from his dais.

But he who really does the dancing,
And he who really does the prancing
(On a horse), has had twice double
Of dance and prance and horse his bellyful.

P.R.

ТАНЦУЕТ ТОТ, КТО НЕ ТАНЦУЕТ

Танцует тот, кто не танцует,
Ножом по рюмочке стучит.
Гарцует тот, кто не гарцует,
С трибуны машет и кричит.

А кто танцует в самом деле
И кто гарцует на коне,
Тем эти пляски надоели,
А эти лошади — вдвойне!

THE HAYSTACK

On a stack of hay, on a southern night
With my face to the firmament, I lay.
                                        Fet

I went up to a stack of hay. It
Seemed to me to be inviting.
I stood and rubbed my shoulder on it:
It was prickly, it was biting.

Its smell was bitter, so its breathing.
It swayed and smoked. Ah, how did Fet
Ever—I wonder—achieve his lying
Down on it? Did he stay quiet?

Insects crawled across my sleeves and
Over my lapels, and steam
Befogged my glasses with an even
Covering of silky film.

I stroked the dust and kissed the friable
Fragments; sought another birth.
But no God above was able
To redeem the pain of life on earth.

Unveiled horror, naked, crushed me,
Numbed my movements as I fell
Down a steep abysmal gulley:
Hopeless, starless, deeply dismal.

The scurrying clouds flew high above me
Crazily and grey with fear.
My palms were sweating and they itched me.
My shirt gave out a sodden glimmer.

СТОГ

Б. Я. Бухштабу

На стоге сена ночью южной
Лицом ко тверди я лежал...
А. Фет

Я к стогу сена подошел.
Он с виду ласковым казался.
Я боком встал, плечом повел,
Так он кололся и кусался.

Он горько пахнул и дышал,
Весь колыхался и дымился.
Не знаю, как на нем лежал
Тяжелый Фет? Не шевелился?

Ползли какие-то жучки
По рукавам и отворотам,
И запотевшие очки
Покрылись шелковым налетом.

Я гладил пыль, ласкал труху,
Я порывался в жизнь иную,
Но бога не было вверху,
Чтоб оправдать тщету земную.

И голый ужас, без одежд,
Сдавив, лишил меня движений.
Я падал в пропасть без надежд,
Без звезд и тайных утешений.

Ополоумев, облака
Летели, серые от страха.
Чесалась потная рука,
Блестела мокрая рубаха.

And, in all that haystack, even
With my back braced up against it,
Not a single straw was given
To check my fall: for me to clutch at.

P.R.

И в целом стоге под рукой,
Хоть всей спиной к нему прижаться,
Соломки не было такой,
Чтоб, ухватившись, задержаться!

On the Moika lived a certain old man.
The mountain of his books I can imagine.
He knew them one and all. All the same
Not for this my friend once summoned me.
Out of the blue in the middle of the day,
Then and there to go and call on him.

For, according to my friend, the meeting
Would bring much joy to both: "You'll hit it off
Immediately. One sorrow and one language
And the shadow of a forgotten poet."

Several times I made the effort,
But rain, business, the late hour,
My moroseness or his mood
Prevented it. And then I heard
He had died. Irrevocably
My visit was annulled. And who
Can tell me it was just postponed?

P.R.

НА МОЙКЕ ЖИЛ ОДИН СТАРИК

На Мойке жил один старик.
Я представляю горы книг.
Он знал того, он знал другого.
Но все равно, не потому
Приятель звал меня к нему
Меж делом, бегло, бестолково.

А потому, что, по словам
Приятеля, обоим нам
Была бы в радость встреча эта.
— Вы б столковались в тот же миг:
Одна печаль, один язык
И тень забытого поэта!

Я собирался много раз,
Но дождь, дела и поздний час,
Я мрачен, он нерасположен.
И вот я слышу: умер он.
Визит мой точно отменен.
И кто мне скажет, что отложен?

WHAT, AGAIN THE GUITAR!

What, again the guitar!
Like a sleeve rolled up!
Opiate of pleasure
Stash it in a cupboard

Let Grigoriev play it
Onwards through the night
As one might expect it
From a swinging Muscovite.

But we with our dry verses,
And with honour, try
In another manner
To cope with our reverses . . .

. . . Smoke from cigarettes
Wind from the canal—
So that none detects
Our furious teardrops fall.

P.R.

ЕЩЕ ЧЕГО, ГИТАРА!

Еще чего, гитара!
Засученный рукав.
Любезная отрава.
Засунь ее за шкаф.

Пускай на ней играет
Григорьев по ночам,
Как это подобает
Разгульным москвичам.

А мы стиху сухому
Привержены с тобой.
И с честью по-другому
Справляемся с бедой.

Дымок от папиросы
Да ветреный канал,
Чтоб злые наши слезы
Никто не увидал.

LAMENT FOR ANNA AKHMATOVA

I

The waves darken at nightfall,
One hears an oarlock rattle.
Charon does not chatter
And she too is still.

Her hands caress the hull,
And as in life her glance
Is steady. Wavelets ripple:
Cocitus and Acheron.

It is ages since this vessel
Carried such a cargo.
The Muse hovers above her
But she is numb:

Elegantly dressed still,
Calm again and young;
As if this last disaster
Were nothing but a chill.

She'd rather take the road
To Compiègne or Paris,
Yet this one, thank the Lord,
Comes as no surprise.

The awe of her encounter
Troubles her a little,
But she breathes no deeper
Than were she still in Tsarskoe.

She floats among the shadows,
The misshapes in the cliffs,
And once as Modigliani
Drew her, so she is.

ПАМЯТИ АННЫ АХМАТОВОЙ

1

Волна темнее к ночи,
Уключина стучит.
Харон неразговорчив,
Но и она — молчит.

Обшивку руки гладят,
А взгляд, как в жизни, тверд.
Пред нею волны катят
Коцит и Ахеронт.

Давно такого груза
Не поднимал челнок.
Летает с криком Муза,
А ей и невдомек.

Опять она нарядна,
Спокойна, молода.
Легка и чуть прохладна
Последняя беда.

Другую бы дорогу,
В Компьен или Париж...
Но этой, слава Богу,
Ее не удивишь.

Свиданьем предстоящим
Взволнована чуть-чуть.
Но дышит грудь не чаще,
Чем в Царском где-нибудь.

Как всякий дух бесплотный
Очерчена штрихом,
Свой путь бесповоротный
Сверяет со стихом.

Плывет она в тумане
Средь чудищ, мимо скал
Такой, как Модильяни
Ее нарисовал.

2

Yesterday after the funeral
I was stung by the blizzard and dreamed
Not of Charon but the croaking
Of ravens. As I sat there,
No bright vision of Lethe
Stirred before me, or other
World but snow and glacial
Cold, and a mound of earth.

Gnawed that night by terror,
My love close by, I lay
Immobile. Death's wing fanned
My forehead. In the darkness
After, trembling still and
Hugging life in my arms,
I stroked Death, hardly breathing.
And a coffin fought with God.

P.R.

2

Вчера, вернувшись с похорон,
Я был метелью опален,
Не снился мне старик Харон,
А снился крик ворон.
Я сел — возник передо мной
Не Леты блеск, не мир иной,
А снег да холод ледяной
Да холмик земляной.

А ночью, ужасом томим,
С подругой рядом, недвижим,
Лежал я. Смерть крылом своим
Мой обвевала лоб.
Потом, во тьме, еще дрожа,
В своих объятьях жизнь держа,
Я смерть ласкал, едва дыша,
И с богом спорил гроб.

Away with these portentous dreams:
There's no excuse for their narration.
The simplest facts of life exceed
Their most unbearable refraction.

When you slumbered, you perceived
Oars and a stone around your neck.
Ah! The chair crept to the bed,
Sadder, infinitely more obscene:

The way it took its stance obliquely;
You would have wept if you had seen,
And remembered, tired, deathly,
How wounded by your friend you'd been.

So why this shrieking—so insane—
Lying in dreams beneath a wheel!
You only have to wake again
To see it all re-done, and real.

P.R.

ЭТИ СНЫ РОКОВЫЕ — ВРАНЬЕ!

Эти сны роковые — вранье!
А рассказчикам нету прощенья,
Потому что простое житье
Безутешней любого смещенья.

Ты увидел, когда ты уснул,
Весла в лодке и камень на шее,
А к постели придвинутый стул
Был печальней в сто раз и страшнее.

По тому, как он косо стоял, —
Ты б заплакал, когда б ты увидел, —
Ты бы вспомнил, как смертно скучал
И как друг тебя горько обидел.

И зачем — непонятно — кричать
В этих снах, под машины ложиться,
Если можно проснуться опять —
И опять это все повторится.

I CLOSE MY EYES AND SEE

I close my eyes and I see
That city in which I live:
Yes, and a faraway roof,
The sun and the Neva's view.

With a clarity sudden and stabbing
I glimpse the day of my fate:
The death throes and the rattle
And the gleam of clouds on the Neva.

God! How we need the immortal
Not for loving or pleasure
But for the joy of the wind
To drive at our backs where it will.

No pain or blame would hurt,
Borne for this easy going:
Ruffled in your coat
Muffled against the wind.

For the joy of this collar turned up
For the joy of the Neva's blue
For this city unique, we can even
In anguish, live life through.

P.R.

ЗАКРОЮ ГЛАЗА И УВИЖУ

Закрою глаза и увижу
Тот город, в котором живу,
Какую-то дальнюю крышу,
И солнце, и вид на Неву.

В каком-то печальном прозренье
Увижу свой день роковой,
Предсмертную боль, и хрипенье,
И блеск облаков над Невой.

О боже, как нужно бессмертье,
Не ради любви и услад,
А ради того, чтобы ветер
Дул в спину и гнал наугад.

Любое стерпеть униженье
Не больно, любую хулу
За легкое это движенье
С замахом полы за полу.

За вечно наставленный ворот,
За синюю невскую прыть,
За этот единственный город,
Где можно и в горе прожить.

THAT WHICH WE DESCRIBE AS SOUL

That which we describe as soul,
Like a cloud is aerial:
Glistens in the shades of night,
Capriciously, recalcitrant;
Or like an aircraft suddenly,
It pricks more subtly than a pin,
Exercising high control
On our life, and rectifying.

Yes, it ranges with the birds,
Streaks cerulean with the sky.
There is no conflagration burns
It, nor rains make dissolute.
That without which none can sigh
And none forgive a poltroon's crack;
That which when we come to die,
Enhancéd we must render back.

Certainly this is the thing
For which no struggle is a sorrow.
It is the glory of our living:
Incontestably excelling;
With old world grace beyond degree . . .
Cloud, soul, little swallow,
I am fettered . . . you are free.

P.R.

ТО, ЧТО МЫ ЗОВЕМ ДУШОЙ

То, что мы зовем душой,
Что, как облако, воздушно
И блестит во тьме ночной
Своенравно, непослушно
Или вдруг, как самолет,
Тоньше колющей булавки,
Корректирует с высот
Нашу жизнь, внося поправки;

То, что с птицей наравне
В синем воздухе мелькает,
Не сгорает на огне,
Под дождем не размокает,
Без чего нельзя вздохнуть,
Ни глупца простить в обиде;
То, что мы должны вернуть,
Умирая, в лучшем виде, —

Это, верно, то и есть,
для чего не жаль стараться,
Что и делает нам честь,
Если честно разобраться.
В самом деле хороша,
Бесконечно старомодна,
Тучка, ласточка, душа!
Я привязан, ты — свободна.

Joseph Alexandrovich Brodsky

Joseph Brodsky is the only contemporary poet from Leningrad whose name is widely known in the West. At the age of twenty-three, in 1963, when he was just becoming known as a poet in his own city, he became the victim of a trial which turned him into a *cause célèbre* both in Leningrad and in the West.

Up to the time of this trial, Brodsky was not different from many young poets of Leningrad; more talented than some, perhaps more definite in his artistic conceptions, but in fact, his name was scarcely known outside his own circle of friends and admirers. His poetry, like that of other young poets, was carefully copied out by hand and circulated "under the coat". He was beginning to read in university dormitories, poetry meetings, and private homes, and he was working wherever he could find work, occasionally as a translator of foreign poetry. Akhmatova knew him and had taken an interest in his poetry.

Then, abruptly, all this changed. On November 29, 1963, in the newspaper *Evening Leningrad*, a lengthy, three-column article appeared. In black headlines, it was titled: "Semi-Literary Parasite". It began:

"A few years ago in the semi-literary circles of Leningrad, a young man appeared calling himself a versifier. He wore velvet pants; in his hands was always the same briefcase, bulging with papers. In the winter, he went about without any covering for his head and the snow freely powdered his red hair.

His friends called him simply, "Osya". But in other circles he was called by the full weight of his name—Joseph Brodsky.

Brodsky frequented the literary groups of beginning poets working in the Culture Palace of the First Five Year Plan. But this versifier in velvet pants decided that working in literary groups was not for his expansive nature. He even began to suggest to the young writers that such study in some way hampered their creativity, and that he, Joseph Brodsky, would scramble up Parnassus in some unique way.

And just how did this self-confident lad wish to arrive in literature? To his account he had twenty—plus perhaps twenty more—verses written by hand in a thin schoolboy's notebook, and all of these verses proclaimed that the author's view of the world was plainly harmful: "The Cemetery", "I Will Die, I Will Die".*

His poetry imitated the poet, propagating pessimism and lack of faith in men. His verses were mixtures of decadentism, pessimism, modernism, and plain babbling. He was not capable of more than this, for he does not possess the strength for independent creation. He has neither sufficient learning nor culture. And what kind of works can come from someone who has not yet completed secondary school?

. . . Having left the literary groups, he began home-made efforts. Brodsky began to exert himself to gain popularity with the young. He rushed to public performances, and from time to time managed to penetrate to the tribune. Several times Brodsky read his verses in the dormitories of Leningrad University, in the Mayakovsky Library, and in the Len-Soviet Palace of Culture. The true lovers of poetry rejected his romances and stanzas. But he was discovered by a bunch of eccentric young ladies and gentlemen, for whom it is always necessary to have something "odd" and "piquant". They were lifted to the heights by means of Joseph Brodsky's verses.

These young gentlemen and ladies congregate around such semi-literary circles. They circle around modish poets, create agitation at their performances, whine after them for autographs. They, and others like them, write down their verses. Thus, some guy who has only barely finished secondary school, on the strength of a few verses, already pretends to call himself a poet.

. . . In this manner one leads the "creative" life. Sleep late. Afterwards, a stroll on the Nevsky. In the Dom Knigi,† a

* Several of the verses quoted in the article were not by Brodsky.

† The largest book store in Leningrad.

little flirtation with the salesgirl in the poetry department, Lucy Levin, the most vital consideration being that he hopes she will provide him with some modish poetical novelty. Later, he proceeds to some editorial office where he knows the standards of creativity are not too exacting.

In the evening a restaurant or café. At a table, a pitcher of cocktails. All around are guests, who are known only by the names of Jeff or Jack, and girls, obligatorily with glasses, obligatorily with long, uncombed hair. So you see, the day goes by. Senselessly! To no one and to nothing is this life useful."

The article proceeds to further and wilder accusations. Brodsky's disreputable friends are listed and described as having borrowed money from their old, widowed mothers. Brodsky is accused of meeting an American and *almost* giving him manuscripts. In addition, he is accused of hatching a hare-brained scheme to leave the country: "In Samarkand, Brodsky tried to accomplish his plan of fleeing the Homeland. Together with . . . [a previously named friend] he went to the airport in order to steal a plane and fly it out of the country, but ascertaining that there was not enough fuel for it to leave the country, they decided to wait for a better occasion."

The article states that Brodsky has been warned repeatedly but that

"Brodsky has not drawn the necessary conclusions. He continues to carry on the same parasitic life. A healthy, 26-year-old lad★ for some four years has done no useful work. He lives on temporary work and in the last resort receives money from his father, a retired photographer-correspondent for a Leningrad newspaper, who, while he does not approve of his son's mode of existence, continues to feed him. Brodsky should take it into his skull to at last begin working, to cease being a parasite on his parents and his fatherland.

. . . Of course it is necessary to cease coddling these semi-literary parasites. For those such as Brodsky there is no room in Leningrad.

★ A three-year mistake in his age; he was only 23 at the time.

What conclusions should be drawn from this story? Not only Brodsky, but all of those who surround him are following the same dangerous path as he. They must be severely warned of this. Let these semi-literary know-nothings receive with Brodsky the most severe response. Let them not muddy the waters!"

This ominous caricature was signed by a trio of names: Ionin, Lerner and Medvedev. The key man was Lerner, a retired secret policeman, who, for unknown reasons, denounced Brodsky to his former colleagues, the secret police. Feeling perhaps that this was not enough, Lerner went to the head of the Leningrad Writers' Union, Alexander Prokofiev, and convinced Prokofiev that, for the good of the city, Brodsky should be expelled from Leningrad. With the help of one cooperative member of the Union, Lerner then arranged to have a unanimous resolution drawn up, stating that Brodsky was "incapable of contributing anything to literature" and that he was writing "anti-Soviet and pornographic verses". It did not matter that none of the members of the group invoked was personally acquainted with Brodsky or his work, or that the head of this particular council, the writer Daniel Granin, was not even informed of their deliberations.

Brodsky was arrested on a charge of *tuneyadstvo*, "social parasitism," a new crime in the Soviet Union under a law enacted only two years before, in 1961.

On February 18, 1964 he was brought to trial in the Dzerzhinsky district of Leningrad. The judge was Mrs Savelieva. There followed this now-famous exchange between the judge and the accused:

Judge: And what is your profession in general?
Brodsky: Poet translator.
J: Who recognized you as a poet? Who enrolled you in the ranks of poets?
B: No one. And who enrolled me in the ranks of humanity?
J: And did you study this?

B: This?

J: To become a poet. You have not tried to enter the university where they give instruction . . . where they study . . . .

B: I did not think . . . I did not think that this was a matter of instruction.

J: What is it then?

B: I think that it is . . . from God.

As the trial progressed, respected members of the Writers' Union stepped forward to defend the young poet. They testified that Brodsky's character was serious and that his work was full of promise. Natalia Grudinina, an editor of poetry anthologies, declared, "The poems which Brodsky wrote in 1959 and 1960, I consider to be the work of a poet in embryo. They still lack polish, but they have a fine originality in their imagery and turn of phrase. Brodsky's translations are on a high professional level." Yefim Etkind, a teacher at the Herzen Institute, and the author of a definitive textbook on style in translations, testified, "I was presented with some of the work of Joseph Brodsky, some translations of the great Polish poet Galczynski. I was struck by the clarity, lyricism and force of Brodsky's verse."

This expert testimony mattered little. Among other witnesses, the prosecution turned up a worker who testified that Brodsky was having a bad influence on his son. "I am the father of a family and know what it is like to have a son who does not work. More than once I have seen my son reading Brodsky's poems. He is a dangerous parasite. We should deal with people like him without pity."

In his peroration, the prosecutor concluded, "Comrade Judges, our great country is in the process of building Communism. A superb opportunity is offered to every Soviet citizen— the pleasure of taking part in a task which is socially useful. The prisoner Brodsky has rejected all ideas of patriotism. He has forgotten the essential principle: He who does not work does not eat. . . . Brodsky should be sent away from this great city of ours. He is a parasite and he is morally disgusting."

A short time later Judge Savelieva read the court's decision which decreed coldly. "It is clear that Brodsky is not a poet. Brodsky is condemned to exile in a remote locality for a period of five years of forced labour."

There were many objections to the decision. During the trial itself, the late Frida Vigdorova, a literary critic and an admirer of Brodsky's work, was present and took stenographic notes of the proceedings. Letters in Brodsky's defence came from Kornei Chukovsky, Samuel Marshak, and Dimitri Shostakovich. While he was still in prison awaiting trial, Anna Akhmatova dedicated a volume of her poetry to him with the words, "To Joseph Brodsky, whose verses seem to me magical." In Leningrad, many humbler people wrote, but all these letters were ignored. Nevertheless, suddenly everyone in Leningrad knew his name. As one young Russian put it, "To be prohibited is to be interesting."

From March 1964 to November 1965, Brodsky lived in exile in the Archangelsk region of northern Russia, doing heavy physical labour, chopping wood and carrying manure. His health suffered. He was offered work by a Moscow publishing house, but he had to refuse. Finally, appeals were made to the Supreme Court of the Russian Federation and he was released without serving out his full term.

Brodsky was famous. In the West, his work was published in quarterlies, anthologies and books. His powerful "Elegy for John Donne," written in 1963, was published by Tri-Quarterly in George Kline's English translation in the spring of 1965, and in 1965 Brodsky wrote "Verses on the Death of T. S. Eliot", modelled on W. H. Auden's "In Memory of W. B. Yeats".

But to date, in his own country, Brodsky has barely been published. Two short poems appeared in *Molodoy Leningrad*, 1966, and two more, including the Eliot poem, in *Den Poezii*, 1967. Some of his poetic translations from English, Polish, Spanish and Serbo-Croatian have appeared in Soviet anthologies. Recently, he has completed translations of Brendan Behan's play, "The Quare Fellow" and Stoppard's "Rosencrantz and Guildenstern are Dead"; perhaps they will be published in the Soviet Union.

It is impossible to know precisely why Brodsky was singled out for so savage an attack; one can only speculate. Further, it is difficult to understand what this attack—which bore so many marks of a personal vendetta—proved. At the time, Brodsky was so little known that an attack on him could scarcely serve as a dramatic warning to other young people. As it turned out, his trial made him famous and far more influential than before. Indeed, rather than acting as a deterrent to other young poets, the trial itself became an embarrassment both at home and abroad. The fact that Brodsky was released after little more than a year indicates that there were some second thoughts, that the affair was regretted. Nevertheless, for obscure reasons, Brodsky is still harrassed. He and his visitors are closely watched. His mail is sometimes diverted. He is not, of course, a member of the Writers' Union and, needless to say, gives no public readings.

In 1970 it was widely rumoured that a book of his poetry would finally be published in his own country, but once again, the plan was cancelled. Although he has been invited to several poetry congresses, he has consistently been refused permission to leave the country. In 1969 he was invited by Robert Lowell and a committee of distinguished poets to read his poems at the meeting of Poetry International in London, and the same year he was asked to appear at the Festival of Two Worlds at Spoleto. The Soviet authorities did not permit him to accept either invitation. Instead, Spoleto officials received an ominously cold reply from a Soviet official saying, "Surprised, not to say puzzled, by the invitation accorded to the so-called poet Brodsky. There is no such poet. True, there was a Brodsky sent to prison a few years ago."

This narrow and provincially unsophisticated attitude is all the more regrettable because a wider display of Brodsky's talents abroad could only inspire respect and admiration for his homeland. In person, he is a philosophical, courteous and contemplative man—the very opposite of the fiery, declaiming agitator. His poetry is unpolitical. Above all, he is an artist.

* * *

The hall was dark. We blinked coming in from the bright sunshine. Brodsky greeted us warmly and led us down the hall to what seemed like a dark ante-room, filled with old furniture and trunks. It was, in fact, half a room, from which he had carved at the back a private nook for himself, using book-shelves piled high with suitcases as separating walls. A small doorway had been created by placing a board between the book-shelves and piling it with two wooden crates and more suitcases. We had to bend down to enter this study-bedroom. It was as if we were entering the captain's cabin on some imaginary ship; it was the cocoon of an intensely private man.

Brodsky is slender, of medium height, with light blue eyes, thinning red hair and fair skin. He was wearing khaki pants, a blue button-down shirt, a black leather belt and small, figured tie. A madras jacket was carelessly draped over the back of the swivel chair in front of his desk which was neatly cluttered with piles of papers and books. His appearance that day came as a surprise to me, for he looked much younger than when I had seen him last. Then, he had seemed taller and heavier; his heavy-lidded eyes and full patriarchal red beard had given him the look of a biblical prophet. But now, clean shaven, wearing Western clothes, with his gay, relaxed manner, he seemed very like some bright young professor at Columbia or Harvard.

In his tiny sanctuary, one feels almost completely cut off from the outside world by the presence of books. They seem every-where, lined up on shelves on every side, from wall to wall and floor to ceiling, surrounding, protecting, insulating. Dictionaries of many languages, volume after volume of Russian poetry, collections of English poets, books of American poetry, they have the warm look of old friends. Among them, carefully placed, are photographs: Robert Frost, Anna Akhmatova, his father in uniform during the war, his parents together, a girl.

Under the single window is Brodsky's bed, used as a couch during the day. His original and whimsical tastes appear in the rows of postcards neatly pinned to the bookshelves (sent by friends from everywhere, mostly Medieval and Renaissance art, except one pink card proclaiming "Beware of Maniac" and another, nestled among the crates: "Stamp out Reality"); in the Chinese characters painted on the crates above his door; in the soft grey fur that covers a chair; in the ceramic fish vase filled with dried flowers hanging above his bed; in the ancient goose-necked lamp on his desk, its lampshade fashioned from the gilded wrapper of a Camels cigarette carton; in a beige poster which announces in bold, black letters: "WANTED DEAD OR ALIVE (Preferably Dead) JOSEPH BRODSKY For Murder, Horse Thieving and Other Acts against the Peace and Dignity of the United States. $25,000 Reward in gold coin."

The whole room is not more than 13 by 9 feet. A visitor to this carefully constructed inner world feels that he is sharing something of the soul of the man who lives there. Yet even in this insulated place, Brodsky complains that is it noisy, that the sound of television penetrates fearfully through the walls, sometimes making it impossible for him to work.

Joseph Brodsky has lived in this same apartment with his parents almost all his life. He was born on May 24, 1940, only a year before the German invasion. His family is Jewish; both parents and grandparents are from Leningrad. His father worked as a photo-journalist for Leningrad newspapers until his retirement. Joseph Brodsky is one of the rare ones who remained and survived the entire 900 days of the Blockade in Leningrad. "I was luckier than many," he says, "because I had my grandparents to care for me." During the war his mother worked as a translator and his father served in the Navy. In 1945-6 his father worked in China as a photo-journalist.

About the Blockade, Brodsky recalls, "I remember that the church on our block was used as a bomb shelter and when I was a small boy we had to go there in the night. It is a Russian custom in the churches to give the priest cards on which are written the names of people to pray for. These cards are kept in special boxes. All these boxes were piled in the cellars and I was put to sleep on them."

Yet although he dismisses it lightly, like all the children of that terrible time he was not left untouched. He was a nervous, high-strung boy. At fifteen he left school at the end of the eighth grade. He worked for a year in a factory and went on geological expeditions. At eighteen, he began to write poetry and tried to

join one of the poetry circles headed by the same Natalia Grudinina who testified at his trial. At the time, she refused, saying that
she had heard that he was "a hysterical lad". Later, at Brodsky's
trial, she admitted, "It was a mistake which I regret. Now I would
gladly accept him in our group and work with him if he wishes."

He had taught himself both English and Polish, and he began
to find occasional work as a translator in publishing houses in
Moscow. He did poetic Russian versions of Spanish, German and
Serbian poetry. His work was good, and he was engaged in
the same slow climb up the literary ladder as other young poets.
Then came the *Evening Leningrad* article and his trial.

Brodsky spends much time in the country outside Leningrad
or in Moscow where he often works and has many friends.
He is an excellent translator of English poetry and has a contract
now for translating a 4,000-line volume of English metaphysical
poetry which, he estimates, will take him two more years to
finish. However, his income from these translations is very
small.

Brodsky has read extensively and deeply in English, Polish
and American poetry, as well as in classical Greek mythology
and religious philosophy (mostly Russian). He considers John
Donne the greatest of lyric poets. He once said that Dostoevsky,
Melville, Joyce, Sterne, Proust and Faulkner were "the greatest
writers of all time". He does not care much for Tolstoy,
Goethe and the French 19th-century novelists. He says that the
Russian poets who have influenced him most are Derzhavin,
Mandelstam, Tsvetayeva, and Pasternak in his later period. He also
has admired the work of a Leningrad contemporary, Vladimir
Ufland, a young poet who wrote and read a great deal in the early
1960's but now is devoting himself to writing children's plays.
For a livelihood, Ufland works as a caretaker in the Geographical
Society.

Brodsky is deeply interested in philosophy and ethics and he
admires and emulates the English metaphysical poets. But his
irony, detachment and coolness are very modern. In Leningrad
it is said as a high compliment that "he writes with the head and
the heart together".

Brodsky is also a religious poet, although not in the sense of church-piety. Pierre Emmanuel of the Académie Française has written: "God, named or unnamed, is everywhere absent-present in the work of the poet. The poetry of Brodsky is religious in a diffuse manner; by awakening constantly with a nostalgic imagery, the question of the reality, without which, and outside of which, all is nothingness." Like Mandelstam and the later Pasternak, but more explicitly than either, Brodsky raises the question of "Christianity and culture". For him this is a live and tormenting issue, as in his "Halt in the Wilderness". George Kline, his translator, says of Brodsky's work: "Brodsky uses slant rhymes, 'compound rhymes' and plays on words. The unit of his poetic construction is the word, rather than the line, and he often groups his powerful individual words into aggregates—complex units of music and meaning—that encompass several lines difficult to translate into English without losing their original flavour."

In Leningrad, Brodsky enjoys a narrower and more selective following than some other poets. He does not arouse the emotions or attract the popular allegiance of Gleb Gorbovsky. Those who admire him—and these include many poets—feel that in his philosophical interests and his mastery of the classical Russian language, he may be the strongest in Leningrad and one of the finest poets in Russia today. Those who do not admire him criticize his work as being "not very Russian" and say they do not entirely understand it.

One thing is certain: Brodsky's work has had a great influence. In Leningrad there is a small company of intellectual followers and disciples who write in his style and have been called "petit-Brodsky". Among those often mentioned are Yevgeny Rein, Anatoly Naiman and Dimitri Bobishev, although Brodsky says modestly, "They were my teachers not my followers." All these poets knew Akhmatova and some of them worked with her. Naiman, for example, worked as her literary secretary and assisted her with some excellent translations of the Italian poet, Leopardi. Naiman and Rein, both now married, live in Moscow where they work as translators. But there are others, including several younger poets now working who are also especially interested in ethics and philosophy and who also often draw their inspiration from the work of Pasternak and Akhmatova. Their work, its spirit, and even its language, is closer and more comprehensible to the Western intellect and academic tradition than the work of other Leningrad poets who look for inspiration and sources almost exclusively in the intricacies of Russian history and language.

Brodsky's self-taught English is remarkably good, although he prefers to speak Russian when discussing poetry and subtle subjects. He chooses his English words carefully, now and then hesitating to look for a specific expression. Sometimes he starts a sentence in English slowly and finishes in a waterfall of rapid Russian. Settling down in his swivel chair in front of the cluttered desk, he talked in his soft voice, ranging over many subjects:

"I liked Leningrad after the war. It had a tired, courageous look that somehow it no longer has, now that everything has been repaired.

"I think the younger generation is better than we, they are cleaner, soberer, perhaps. And"—he added with a characteristic touch of wry humour—"they have better teeth.

"Sometimes," he said wistfully, "I think that France, England, and all those countries exist only on the pages of geography books.

"Fame? I think perhaps it is bad in a way for poets to be too famous, to have publicity. It changes the atmosphere. The only thing that counts in poetry is what happens between the reader, alone, and the poet. Nothing else is important.

"Everyone must find his own way in his own place. This takes sometimes a special kind of courage."

Of his imprisonment, he says only: "I am wiser now."

Even of love, he talks and writes with wry irony rather than passion, as in these lines from "Adieu, Mademoiselle Véronique":

You'll forgive me, I'm sure, for this air of jesting.
It seemed the best method to save strong feelings
from masses of weak ones.

This detachment and intellectuality might seem cold if it were not tempered by his endearing modesty and gentleness. His warmth and sense of fun often lead him to make jokes at his own expense. He rummaged through a drawer looking for snapshots; his favourite pictures of himself are those showing him wearing an over-sized checked cap or a silly expression. Brodsky's friends are devoted to him almost as much for these personal characteristics as for his art. They delight in his wonderful coffee, strong and pungent, a rare thing in a tea-drinking country. He grinds and carefully prepares it himself. They love his jokes and witty conversation. When he writes to friends abroad, he signs himself puckishly, "From Russia, with love".

At dawn we left Brodsky's apartment and walked in the freshly-washed streets of Leningrad. The pearl sky of the White Nights was reflected in the streets in pink, blue and gold. At the end of the street, we turned to walk along the Summer Garden, green and rustling with the birds singing. Brodsky recited one of the English limericks which he likes to compose. This one began, "Our Russia's a country of birches, and axes and ikons and churches". We talked of the green hills of Massachusetts. We parted on a bridge. The newly-restored black lamp-posts with their graceful lanterns were crested with golden eagles and arrows pointing East, West, North and South. Brodsky said, "Relax, care for yourself. Come back, you will always find me here." Then, with a jaunty wave he turned and went back over the bridge.

Editor's Note

In June, 1972, as this book was being printed, Joseph Brodsky was compelled to leave his country. He is presently planning to live and work in the United States.

S.M.

A HALT IN THE WILDERNESS

So few Greeks live in Leningrad today
that we have razed a Greek church, to make space
for a new concert hall, built in today's
grim and unhappy style. And yet a concert hall with more than fifteen hundred seats
is not so grim a thing. And who's to blame
If virtuosity has more appeal
than the worn banners of an ancient faith?
Still, it is sad that from this distance now
we see, not the familiar onion-domes,
but a grotesquely flattened silhouette.
Yet men are not so heavily in debt
to the grim ugliness of balanced forms
as to the balanced forms of ugliness.

I well remember how the church succumbed.
I was then making frequent springtime calls
at the home of a Tartar family
who lived nearby. From their front window, one
could clearly see the outline of the church.
It started in the midst of Tartar talk,
but soon the racket forced its rumbling way
into our conversation, mingling with,
then drowning out, our steady human speech.
A huge power shovel clanked up to the church,
an iron ball dangling from its boom, and soon
the walls began to give way peaceably.
Not to give way would be ridiculous
for a church wall in face of such a foe.
Moreover, the power shovel may have thought
the wall a dead and soulless thing and thus,

ОСТАНОВКА В ПУСТЫНЕ

Теперь так мало греков в Ленинграде,
что мы сломали Греческую церковь,
дабы построить на свободном месте
концертный зал. В такой архитектуре
есть что-то безнадежное. А впрочем,
концертный зал на тыщу с лишним мест
не так уж безнадежен: это — храм,
и храм искусства. Кто же виноват,
что мастерство вокальное дает
сбор больший, чем знамена веры?
Жаль только, что теперь издалека
мы будем видеть не нормальный купол,
а безобразно плоскую черту.
Но что до безобразия пропорций,
то человек зависит не от них,
а чаще от пропорций безобразья.

Прекрасно помню, как ее ломали.
Была весна, и я как раз тогда
ходил в одно татарское семейство,
неподалеку жившее. Смотрел
в окно и видел Греческую церковь.
Всё началось с татарских разговоров;
а после в разговор вмешались звуки,
сливавшиеся с речью поначалу,
но вскоре — заглушившие ее.
В церковный садик въехал экскаватор
с подвешенной к стреле чугунной гирей.
И стены стали тихо поддаваться.
Смешно не поддаваться, если ты
стена, а пред тобою — разрушитель.
К тому же, экскаватор мог считать
ее предметом неодушевленным

to a degree, like its own self. And in
the universe of dead and soulless things
resistance is regarded as bad form.
Next came the dump trucks, then the bulldozers . . .
So, in the end, I sat—late that same night—
among fresh ruins in the church's apse.
Night yawned behind the altar's gaping holes.
And through these open altar-wounds I watched
retreating streetcars as they slowly swam
past phalanxes of deathly-pale streetlamps.
I saw now through the prism of that church
a swarm of things that churches do not show.

Some day, when you and I no longer are,
or rather, after we have been, there will
spring up in what was once our space
a thing of such a kind as will bring fear,
a panic fear, to those who knew us best.
But those who knew us will be very few.
The dogs, moved by old memory, still lift
their hindlegs at a once familiar spot.
The church's walls have long since been torn down,
but these dogs see the church walls in their dreams—
dreams that are criss-crossed with the waking world.
Perhaps the earth still holds that ancient smell:
asphalt can't cover up what a dog sniffs.
What can this building be to such as dogs!
For them the church still stands; they see it plain.
And what to people is a patent fact
leaves them entirely cold. This quality
is sometimes called "a dog's fidelity."
And if I were to speak in earnest of
the "relay race of human history,"
I'd swear by nothing but this relay race—
this race of all the generations who
have sniffed, and who will sniff, the ancient smells.

и, до известной степени, подобным
себе. А в неодушевленном мире
не принято давать друг другу сдачи.
Потом — туда согнали самосвалы,
бульдозеры... И как-то в поздний час
сидел я на развалинах абсиды.
В провалах алтаря зияла ночь.
И я — сквозь эти дыры в алтаре —
смотрел на убегавшие трамваи,
на вереницу тусклых фонарей.
И то, чего вообще не встретишь в церкви,
теперь я видел через призму церкви.

Когда-нибудь, когда не станет нас,
точнее — после нас, на нашем месте
возникнет тоже что-нибудь такое,
чему любой, кто знал нас, ужаснется.
Но знавших нас не будет слишком много.
Вот так, по старой памяти, собаки
на прежнем месте задирают лапу.
Ограда снесена давным-давно,
но им, должно быть, грезится ограда.
Их грезы перечеркивают явь.
А может быть земля хранит тот запах:
асфальту не осилить запах псины.
И что им этот безобразный дом!
Для них тут садик, говорят вам — садик.
А то, что очевидно для людей,
собакам совершенно безразлично.
Вот это и зовут: «собачья верность».
И если довелось мне говорить
всерьез об эстафете поколений,
то верю только в эту эстафету.
Вернее, в тех, кто ощущает запах.

Так мало нынче в Ленинграде греков,
да и вообще — вне Греции — их мало.

So few Greeks live in Leningrad today,
outside of Greece, in general, so few—
too few to save the buildings of the faith.
And to have faith in buildings—none asks that.
It is one thing to bring a folk to Christ;
to bear His cross is something else again.
Their duty was a single thing and clear,
but they lacked strength to live that duty whole.
Their unploughed fields grew thick with vagrant weeds.
"Thou who doest sow, keep thy sharp plough at hand
and we shall tell thee when thy grain is ripe."
They failed to keep their sharp ploughs close at hand.

Tonight I stare into the window's void
and think about that point to which we've come,
and if then I ask myself: from which are we
now most remote—the world of ancient Greece,
or Orthodoxy? Which is closest now?
What lies ahead? Does a new epoch wait
for us? And, if it does, what duty do we owe?—
What sacrifices must we make for it?

По крайней мере, мало для того,
чтоб сохранить сооруженья веры.
А верить в то, что мы сооружаем
от них никто не требует. Одно,
должно быть, дело нацию крестить,
а крест нести — уже совсем другое.
У них одна обязанность была.
Они ее исполнить не сумели.
Непаханное поле заросло.
«Ты, сеятель, храни свою соху,
а мы решим, когда нам колоситься».
Они свою соху не сохранили.

Сегодня ночью я смотрю в окно
и думаю о том, куда зашли мы?
И от чего мы больше далеки:
от православья или эллинизма?
К чему близки мы? Что там, впереди?
Не ждет ли нас теперь другая эра?
И если так, то в чем наш общий долг?
И что должны мы принести ей в жертву?

TO A CERTAIN POETESS

I have a touch of normal classicism
and you, my dear, a bad case of sarcasm.
A woman whose career involves sales taxes
is apt to give in to her own caprice.
You've seen an "iron age" in our present epoch.
But I had never dreamed (to change the topic)
that I, whose soberness of style was classic,
would balance on the thin edge of a knife.

It seems that death-of-friendship now has struck us.
This is the start of an extended ruckus.
Yet you can blame no one except old Bacchus
if you should lack advancement in your job.
I am the same now, leaving this arena,
as when I entered it. Yet I stand in a
shroud of volcanic ash, like Herculaneum,
and cannot lift a hand to help you out.

So let us call it quits. I've lost my freedom.
I eat potatoes; I sleep in a hay-barn.
On this thief's head, I may report, no hat's worn:
what shows there is the glow of a bald spot.
I am a parrot, a mere imitator.
The parrot-life is hidden well away, dear.
But when the Law put me in its disfavour
your bright predictions warmed my battered heart.

There are some things forbidden by the Muses
to those who serve them. Yet the Muses' service
fills poets' fingers with a holy tremor.
None then can doubt God's presence or His power.
One "poet" sits preparing memoranda.
Another sighs, muffling a murmur. And a
third, following a well-rehearsed agenda,
plucks lines from other poets like spring flowers.

ОДНОЙ ПОЭТЕССЕ

Я заражен нормальным классицизмом.
А вы, мой друг, заражены сарказмом.
Конечно, просто сделаться капризным,
по ведомству акцизному служа.
К тому ж, вы звали этот век железным.
Но я не думал, говоря о разном,
что, зараженный классицизмом трезвым,
я сам гулял по острию ножа.

Теперь конец моей и вашей дружбе.
Зато начало многолетней тяжбе.
Теперь и вам продвинуться по службе
мешает Бахус, но никто другой.
Я оставляю эту ниву тем же,
каким взошел я на нее. Но так же
я затвердел, как Геркуланум в пемзе.
И я для вас не шевельну рукой.

Оставим счеты. Я давно в неволе.
Картофель ем и сплю на сеновале.
Могу прибавить, что теперь на воре
уже не шапка — лысина горит.
Я, эпигон и попугай. Не вы ли
жизнь попугая от себя скрывали.
Когда мне вышли от закона «вилы»,
я вашим прорицаньем был согрет.

Служенье Муз чего-то там не терпит.
Зато само обычно так торопит,
что по рукам бежит священный трепет
и несомненна близость Божества.
Один певец подготовляет рапорт.
Другой рождает приглушенный ропот.
А третий знает, что он сам лишь рупор.
И он срывает все цветы родства.

Death surely will make plain that mere sarcasm
can't keep up with life's energy. Its prism
can only magnify life's cytoplasm.
Alas, it can't illuminate life's core.
Thus, bound in long-term service to the Muse, I
prefer the classic to the mere sarcastic,
although I, like the Syracusan mystic,
might view the world from a deep barrel's floor.

Let's call it quits. A sign, no doubt, of flabbiness.
Foreseeing your sarcastic lack of sadness,
in this remote place, I would bless non-drabness:
the blindingly bright buzzing of a wasp
above a simple daisy can unnerve me.
I see the sheer abyss that lies before me.
My consciousness whirls like a spinning fanwheel
about the steady axis of the past.

The shoemaker builds boots. The busy baker
produces pretzels. And the necromancer
leafs through huge folio-volumes. So the sinner
makes special efforts, sinning every day.
A porpoise tows a tripod through the billows.
Those things that seemed most real to old Apollo's
calm glance will prove, at last, most hollow.
The forests roar, but the high heavens are deaf.

Autumn will soon be with us. In briefcases
school notebooks find their nest. And enchantresses
like you with care pile up their braided tresses
into a shield against the wind's cold knife.
I recollect our trip to the Crimea,
when both of us loved nature, loved to see a
wild landscape—the more beautiful the freer.
I am astonished, madam, and I grieve.

И скажет смерть, что не поспеть сарказму
за силой жизни. Проницая призму,
способен он лишь увеличить плазму.
Ему, увы, не озарить ядра.
И вот, столь долго состоя при Музах,
я отдал предпочтенье классицизму.
Хоть я и мог, как мистик в Сиракузах,
взирать на мир из глубины ведра.

Оставим счеты. Вероятно, слабость.
Я, предвкушая ваш сарказм и радость,
в своей глуши благословляю разность:
жужжанье ослепительной осы
в простой ромашке вызывает робость.
Я сознаю, что предо мною пропасть.
И крутится сознание, как лопасть
вокруг своей негнущейся оси.

Сапожник строит сапоги. Пирожник
сооружает крендель. Чернокнижник
листает толстый фолиант. А грешник
усугубляет, что ни день, грехи.
Влекут дельфины по волнам треножник,
и Аполлон обозревает ближних —
в конечном счете, безгранично внешних.
Шумят леса, и небеса глухи.

Уж скоро осень. Школьные тетради
лежат в портфелях. Чаровницы, вроде
вас, по утрам укладывают пряди
в большой пучок, готовясь к холодам.
Я вспоминаю эпизод в Тавриде,
наш обоюдный интерес к природе.
Всегда в ее дикорастущем виде.
И удивляюсь, и грущу, мадам.

ADIEU, MADEMOISELLE VERONIQUE

I

If I end my days in my love's winged shelter,
which well may be, since war's meat-grinder
is a luxury-item of lesser nations,
since, after manifold combinations,
Mars has moved closer to palms and cacti,
and I myself couldn't hurt a housefly,
not even in summer, its houseflown heyday—
in short, if I do not die from a bullet,
if I die, pyjama'd, on my own pillow,
since the land of my birth is a major power—

II

—in some twenty years, when my own children,
being no longer able to make a living
by trading on reflections of my laurels,
start to earn their own way—I shall be so bold as
to leave my own family—in twenty seasons.
Under watch and ward for my loss of reason,
I shall go, if my strength holds out, to the building
that has a pharmacy on the corner,
to find the one thing in the whole of Russia
that brings you to my mind—even though I'm breaking
the rule: don't go back for what others abandon.

III

In manners and morals this counts as progress.
In some twenty years I shall fetch the armchair
that you sat on, facing me, when, for Christ's body,
the cross's torments at last were ended—
you sat, on that fifth day of Holy Week, folding
your arms, like Napoleon exiled on Elba.
Palm fronds glowed golden at every crossing.
You laid down your arms on your grass-green garment,
avoiding the open-armed risk of passion.

ПРОЩАЙТЕ, МАДМУАЗЕЛЬ ВЕРОНИКА

I

Если кончу дни под крылом голубки,
что вполне реально, раз мясорубки
становятся роскошью малых наций —
после множества комбинаций
Марс перемещается ближе к пальмам;
а сам я мухи не трону пальцем
даже в ее апогей, в июле —
словом, если я не умру от пули,
если умру в постели, в пижаме,
ибо принадлежу к великой державе,

II

то лет через двадцать, когда мой отпрыск,
не сумев отоварить лавровый отблеск,
сможет сам зарабатывать, я осмелюсь
бросить свое семейство — через
двадцать лет, окружен опекой
по причине безумия, в дом с аптекой
я приду пешком, если хватит силы,
за единственным, что о тебе в России
мне напомнит. Хоть против правил
возвращаться за тем, что другой оставил.

III

Это в сфере нравов сочтут прогрессом.
Через двадцать лет я приду за креслом,
на котором ты предо мной сидела
в день, когда для Христова тела
завершались распятья муки —
в пятый день Страстной ты сидела, руки
скрестив, как Буонапарт на Эльбе.
И на всех перекрестках белели вербы.
Ты сложила руки на зелень платья,
не рискуя их раскрывать в объятья.

IV

A pose such as yours, though not so intended,
is a most fitting symbol of man's existence.
This is not, by any means, immobility.
It's an apotheosis of men as objects,
replacing submissiveness with mere quiet.
This is a new kind of Christian teaching:
one has a duty to guard and cherish
those who consider themselves dead objects,
who won't even wake from their deathlike quiet
at the final sounding of Gabriel's trumpet.

V

It's a habit with prophets to be unhealthy.
Most seers are cripples. To put it briefly,
I am no more a seer than crafty Calchas.
To prophesy is to lift a cactus,
or a lion's jaws, to a helmet-visor.
It's like learning in Braille your alpha-beta.
A hopeless task. To my groping fingers
there are very few objects that feel much like you
in this empty world. Even your own victims
will tell the same tale as your oracle's visions.

VI

You'll forgive me, I'm sure, for this air of jesting.
It seemed the best method to save strong feelings
from masses of weak ones. The mode of masking,
which comes from the Greeks, is again in fashion.
At the present time it's the strong who perish,
while the tribes of the weak multiply both wholesale
and retail. Take this as my up-to-dating,
my subtle *postscriptum* to Darwin's teaching
(his theory is already stiff and cracking);
consider this as the new jungle justice.

IV

Данная поза, при всей приязни,
это лучшая гемма для нашей жизни.
И она отнюдь не недвижность. Это —
апофеоз в нас самих предмета.
Замена смиренья простым покоем.
То-есть, новый вид Христианства, коим
долг дорожить и стоять на страже
тех, кто, должно быть, способен даже
когда придет Гавриил с трубою,
мертвый предмет продолжать собою!

V

У пророков не принято быть здоровым.
Прорицатели в массе увечны. Словом,
я не более зряч, чем назонов Калхас.
Потому — прорицать все равно, что кактус
или львиный зев подносить к забралу.
Всё равно, что учить алфавит по Брайлю.
Безнадежно. Предметов, по крайней мере,
на тебя похожих наощупь в мире,
что называется, кот наплакал.
Каковы твои жертвы, таков оракул.

VI

Ты, несомненно, простишь мне этот
гаерский тон. Это — лучший метод
сильные чувства спасти от массы
слабых. Греческий принцип маски
снова в ходу. Ибо в наше время
сильные гибнут. Тогда как племя
слабых плодится, и врозь, и оптом.
Прими же сегодня, как мой постскриптум
к теории Дарвина, столь пожухлой,
эту новую правду джунглей.

VII

In some twenty years, for to call to mind what
is absent is easier than to make it
good by supplying a thing that's novel
—the absence of law is much worse than your absence—
I shall stare my fill like some modern Gogol,
never glancing back, having no misgivings,
as the magic lantern of Christ's own passion,
at the sound of drops from the dripping faucet,
lights up the back of the empty armchair
as though it were meant for a movie screening.

VIII

In our past there is greatness—but prose in our future.
For one asks no more from an empty armchair
than one would ask from you who once sat upon it
as calm as the waters of Lago di Garda,
crossing your arms, as I've already written.
The sum total of all of today's embraces
gives far less of love than the outstretched arms of
Christ on the cross. This lame poet's★ finding
looms before me in Holy Week, '67,
blocking my leap to the 1990's.

IX

If that bird lays no egg and thus fails to save me,
so that I'm left alone in this labyrinthine
retreat, without help from my Ariadne
(for death can have variants, and it's valor
in men to foreknow them), alas, my fate is
to be worthy of being denounced and sentenced
to a term in a work-camp, and dysentery—
but if only it isn't a lie they've told me,
and old Lazarus rose from the dead in truth, then
I too shall rise, rushing for that armchair.

★ The "lame poet" is Boris Pasternak.

VII

Через двадцать лет — ибо легче вспомнить
то, что отсутствует, чем восполнить
это чем-то иным снаружи.
Ибо отсутствие права хуже,
чем твое отсутствие — новый Гоголь,
насмотреться сумею, бесспорно, вдоволь,
без оглядки вспять, без былой опаски, —
как волшебный фонарь Христовой Пасхи
оживляет под звуки воды из крана
спинку кресла пустого, как холст экрана.

VIII

В нашем прошлом величье, в грядущем — проза.
Ибо с кресла пустого не больше спроса,
чем с тебя, в нем сидевшей ЛаГарды тише,
руки сложив, как писал я выше.
Впрочем, в сумме своей наших дней объятья
много меньше раскинутых рук распятья.
Так что эта находка певца хромого
сейчас, на Страстной Шестьдесят Седьмого,
предо мной маячит подобьем вето
на прыжки в девяностые годы века.

IX

Если меня не спасет та птичка,
то-есть, если она не снесет яичка
и в сем лабиринте без Ариадны
(ибо у смерти есть варианты,
предвидеть которые — тоже доблесть)
я останусь один и, увы, сподоблюсь
холеры, доноса, отправки в лагерь —
то если только не ложь, что Лазарь
был воскрешен, то я сам воскресну.
Тем скорее, знаешь, приближусь к креслу.

X

But rushing is stupid and sinful. *Vale*!
That is, there is no place to rush to. Surely
so sturdy an armchair can't be disabled.
Here in the East we use chairs and tables
for three generations, not counting losses
from fire and from theft. But the worst of all is
the thought that the chair might be dumped together
with others in storage. If this should ever
take place, I would carve in plain wood a picture
of my dove-like beloved, and her mate with her.

XI

Your armchair will arc like a bee bound hive-ward
within the night orbits of chairs and tables.
Labels create a new astrophysics,
which has been—and here it is wise to whisper—
confirmed by long practice of jails and drill-fields:
whatever is branded or fixed with labels
provides a firm basis for views unswerving,
and this will apply to both dead and living.
I shall not search—a homesick Ulysses—
for armchairs like yours, or familiar faces.

XII

I am not a collector of relics, really.
Keep in mind, if this discourse seems long, that freely
to speak of an armchair is but a reason
for penetrating to other regions.
Great faiths leave behind only holy relics.
Judge then of the vast power of love, if objects
touched by you I now hold, while you live, as holy.
But note: what such practices prove is only
that the poet was born in a major power;
they prove nothing concerning the poet's lyre.

X

Впрочем, спешка глупа и греховна. *Vale!*
То-есть некуда так поспешать. Едва ли
может крепкому креслу грозить погибель.
Ибо у нас, на Востоке, мебель
служит трем поколеньям кряду.
А я исключаю пожар и кражу.
Страшней, что смешать его могут с кучей
других при уборке. На этот случай
я даже сделать готов зарубки,
изобразив голубка́ голу́бки.

XI

Пусть теперь кружит, как пчелы ульев,
по общим орбитам столов и стульев
кресло твое по ночной столовой.
Клеймо — не позор, а основа новой
астрономии, что — перейдем на шопот —
подтверждает армейско-тюремный опыт:
заклейменные вещи — источник твердых
взглядов на мир у живых и мертвых.
Так что мне не взирать, как в подобны лица,
на похожие кресла с тоской Улисса.

XII

Я — не сборщик реликвий. Подумай, если
эта речь длинновата, что речь о кресле
только повод проникнуть в другие сферы.
Ибо от всякой великой веры
остаются, как правило, только мощи.
Так суди же о силе любви, коль вещи
те, к которым ты прикоснулась ныне,
превращаю — при жизни твоей — в святыни.
Посмотри: доказуют такие нравы
не величье певца, но его державы.

XIII

The eagle of Russia without its crown is
no more than a crow. And a muttered groan is
all that remains of its once-proud screaming.
This is old age in eagles; the voice of feeling
has turned to an echo or shade of power.
And love-songs are pitched but a little lower.
For love, clearly, is an imperial passion,
and you, are one whom—to her great good fortune—
Russia must address in imperial accents,
recovering her lost imperial stature.

XIV

The armchair is quietly drinking warmness
from the anteroom. Water drips from the faucet,
drop by drop, as it splashes into the washstand.
An alarm clock chirps modestly near the nightlamp.
The flat empty walls share an even lighting
with flowers by the window, whose shadows are fighting
to push the room out through the window's structure.
All this taken together is—now—a picture
of the distant and near, of the deep and shallow,
before we existed.—And what will follow.

XV

I wish you good night. May my own night be not
sleepless. And you, won't you bid a good night to
my country for settling accounts with me—from
that far place where, seemingly, by a simple
miracle—or is it sheer massed miles?—you're
only a postal address. The trees roar
by the window; roof silhouettes mark out day's end.
In one's motionless body the mind flings open
occasional doors in one's hand, like doors to
a furnace. I start. Then my pen pursues you.

246

XIII

Русский орел, потеряв корону,
напоминает сейчас ворону.
Его, горделивый недавно, клекот
теперь превратился в картавый рокот.
Это — старость орлов или — голос страсти
обернувшейся следствием, эхом власти.
И любовная песня — немногим тише.
Любовь — имперское чувство. Ты же
такова, что Россия, к своей удаче,
говорить не может с тобой иначе.

XIV

Кресло стоит и вбирает теплый
воздух прихожей. В стояк за каплей
падает капля из крана. Скромно
стрекочет будильник под лампой. Ровно
падает свет на пустые стены
и на цветы у окна, чьи тени
стремятся за раму продлить квартиру.
И вместе всё создает картину
того в этот миг — и вдали, и возле —
как было до нас. И как будет после.

XV

Доброй ночи тебе, да и мне — не бденья.
Доброй ночи стране моей для сведенья
личных счетов со мной пожелай оттуда,
где посредством верст или просто чуда
ты превратишься в почтовый адрес.
Деревья шумят за окном, и абрис
крыш представляет границу суток...
В неподвижном теле порой рассудок
открывает в руке, как в печи, заслонку.
И перо за тобою бежит вдогонку.

XVI

My pen cannot reach you. You're cloudlike, fleeting.
The shape of a girl, for each man, is surely
his soul's shape—you, Muse can confirm this richly—
implying love's source but, alas, love's ruin,
for souls have no bodies. Which means that you are
still farther away. And my pen cannot reach you.
So give me your hand as we part. That's better
than nothing. Our parting is solemn, lofty,
since it is forever. The zither's silent.

Forever is not a word, but a number
whose unending zeroes, when grass grows above us,
will stretch out beyond our small time, our epoch.

Не догонит!.. Поелику ты как облак.
То-есть, облик девы, конечно, облик
души для мужчины. Не так ли, Муза?
В этом причины и смерть союза.
Ибо души — бесплотны. Ну что ж. Тем дальше
ты от меня. Не догонит!.. Дай же
на прощание руку. На том спасибо.
Величава наша разлука, ибо
навсегда расстаемся. Смолкает цитра.
Навсегда — не слово, а вправду цифра,

чьи нули, когда мы зарастем травою,
перекроют эпоху и век с лихвою.

NEW STANZAS TO AUGUSTA★

To M.B.

1

September came on Tuesday.
It poured all night.
The birds had all flown south.
I was so much alone, so brave,
I did not even watch them go.
The empty sky is broken now;
rain-curtains close the last clear spot.
I do not need the south.

2

Buried alive here,
I wade through twilight stubble.
My boots churn up the field
(Thursday blusters above my head),
but the cut stalks stand erect,
feeling almost no pain.
Switches of pussywillow
plunge a pinkish headland
into the swamp where the guard has been lifted,
muttering something as they upset
a nest of shrikes.

3

Kick and slosh, swirl and gurgle.
I do not quicken my steps.
Quench and snuff out
the spark you know so well.

★ This poem was written during the first year of Brodsky's exile in a remote northern region of Russia: the province of Archangelsk. The title refers to Byron's "Stanzas to Augusta" (which Pasternak had translated into Russian): in both cases an exiled poet addresses a loved woman who remains behind —in Byron's case, his sister; in Brodsky's, "M.B.", to whom the poem is dedicated. *G.L.K.*

НОВЫЕ СТАНСЫ К АВГУСТЕ

М. Б.

1

Во вторник начался сентябрь.
Дождь лил всю ночь.
Все птицы улетели прочь.
Лишь я так одинок и храбр,
что даже не смотрел им вслед.
Пустынный небосвод разрушен.
Дождь стягивает просвет.
Мне юг не нужен.

2

Тут, захороненный живьем,
я в сумерках брожу жнивьем.
Сапог мой разрывает поле
(бушует надо мной четверг),
но срезанные стебли лезут вверх,
почти не ощущая боли.
А прутья верб,
вонзая розоватый мыс
в болото, где снята охрана,
бормочут, опрокидывая вниз
гнездо жулана.

3

Стучи и хлюпай, пузырись, шурши.
Я шаг свой не убыстрю.
Известную тебе лишь искру
гаси, туши.

My frozen hands pressed to my hips,
I roam from mound to hillock—
without memories, with only an inner noise,
kicking my bootsoles against the rocks.
I bend down over a dark stream,
and recoil in shock.

4

What does it matter that a shadow of mindlessness
has crossed my eyes, that the damp
has soaked my beard, that my cap, askew,
—a crown for this twilight—is reflected
like some boundary beyond which
my soul cannot penetrate?
I do not try to get beyond my visor,
buttons, collar, boots, or cuffs.
But my heart pounds suddenly when I discover
that somewhere I am torn. The cold
crashes into my chest, jolting my heart.

5

The water mutters ahead of me,
and the frost reaches out for the slit of my mouth.
With more than a slit one cannot breathe:
It's not a face but the scene
of a landslide.
My laugh is twisted;
it brings terror to the brushwood path
that cuts across the twilight swamp.
A gust of rain
atomizes the darkness.
My shadow runs, like a thing alive,
from these reddened eyelids, galloping
on waveback under pines and weeping willows.
It loses itself among its shadowy doubles
as I could never do.

Замерзшую ладонь прижав к бедру,
бреду я от бугра к бугру,
без памяти, с одним каким-то звуком,
подошвой по камням стучу.
Склоняясь к темному ручью,
гляжу с испугом.

4

Что ж, пусть легла бессмысленности тень
в моих глазах, и пусть впиталась сырость
мне в бороду, и кепка — набекрень —
венчая этот сумрак, отразилась,
как та черта, которую душе
не перейти —
я не стремлюсь уже
за козырек, за пуговку, за ворот,
за свой сапог, за свой рукав.
Лишь сердце вдруг забьется, отыскав,
что где-то я пропорот. Холод
трясет его, мне ь грудь попав.

5

Бормочет предо мной вода,
и тянется мороз в прореху рта.
Иначе и не вымолвить: чем может
быть не лицо, а место, где обрыв
произошел?
И смех мой крив
и сумрачную гать тревожит.
И крошит темноту дождя порыв.
И образ мой второй, как человек,
бежит от красноватых век,
подскакивает на волне
под соснами, потом под ивняками,
мешается с другими двойниками,
как никогда не затеряться мне.

6

Beat and slosh. Chew into the rotted bridge.
The flooded ditches by the country churchyard
suck colour from the wooden crosses.
But even the leaves of grass
cannot tinge this swamp with blue.
Trample the oat-barns.
Rage through the still-thick foliage.
Penetrate to the root depths
and rouse all the dead men, all the ghosts,
there, in the earth, and here, in my heart.
Let them escape, cutting corners as they run,
across the stubble, into the emptied villages;
let them wave their scarecrow hats to greet
arriving autumn days—abrupt like landed birds.

7

Here on the hills, under empty skies,
among roads which end in forests,
life steps back from itself
and stares astonished at the forms
which hiss and roar around it. Roots
cling, wheezing, to your boots,
and all the village fires are spent.
Here I wander in a no man's land
and take a lease on non-existence.
Wind tears the warmth out of my hands.
A tree-hollow douses me with water;
mud twists the ribbon of the footpath.

8

It's as though I'm not really here,
but somewhere on the sidelines, somewhere overboard.
The stubble swells and points straight up
like a corpse's beard;
on the shrike's nest that lies in the grass
a riot of ants boils with indignation.

6

Стучи и хлюпай. Жуй подгнивший мост.
Пусть хляби, окружив погост,
высасывают краску крестовины.
Но даже этак кончиком травы
болоту не прибавить синевы...
Топчи овины,
бушуй среди густой еще листвы.
Вторгайся по корням в глубины
и там, в земле, как здесь, в моей груди
всех призраков и мертвецов буди.
И пусть они бегут, срезая угол,
по жниву к опустевшим деревням
и машут налетевшим дням,
как шляпы пугал.

7

Здесь на холмах, среди пустых небес,
среди дорог, ведущих только в лес,
жизнь отступает от самой себя
и смотрит с изумлением на формы,
шумящие вокруг. И корни
вцепляются в сапог, сопя,
и гаснут все огни в селе.
И вот бреду я по ничьей земле
и у Небытия прошу аренду.
И ветер рвет из рук моих тепло,
и плещет надо мной водой дупло,
и скручивает грязь тропинки ленту.

8

Да здесь как будто вправду нет меня.
Я где-то в стороне, за бортом.
Топорщится и лезет вверх стерня,
как волосы на теле мертвом,
и над гнездом, в траве простертом,
вскипает муравьев возня.

Nature settles its accounts with the past
in the same old way. But her face,
even when flooded with sunset light,
betrays her malice.
With all five of my senses
I shove off from the forest.
No, Lord! My eyes are clouded;
I shall not sit in judgment.
And if—to my misfortune—
I prove unable to control myself,
then, oh God, hack off my hands
as though I were a thieving Finn.

9

Pollux, dear friend. All merges to a stain.
No groan shall be wrenched from my lips.
Here I stand, my coat thrown open,
letting the world flow into my eyes
through a sieve of incomprehension.
I'm nearly deaf. O God, I'm nearly blind.
I hear no words, and the moon burns
steadily at no more than twenty watts. I will not set my
    course
across the sky between the stars or rain drops.
The woods will echo
not with my songs, but only with my coughs.

10

September now. And night. My only
company a candle. A shadow
peers over my shoulder at these papers,
swarming among the torn-up roots.
An apparition of you rustles
among the shadows, gurgling in the water,
smiling starlike in the open doorway.

Природа расправляется с былым,
как водится. Но лик ее при этом
пусть залитый закатным светом
невольно делается злым.
И всею пятернею чувств — пятью
отталкиваюсь я от леса:
нет, Господи! в глазах завеса
и я не превращусь в судью.
И если — на беду свою —
я всё-таки с собой не слажу,
Ты, Боже, отруби ладонь мою,
как финн за кражу.

9

Друг Полидевк. Тут всё слилось в пятно.
Из уст моих не вырвется стенанье.
Вот я стою в распахнутом пальто
и мир течет в глаза сквозь решето,
сквозь решето непониманья.
Я глуховат. Я, Боже, слеповат.
Не слышу слов, и ровно в двадцать ватт
горит луна. Пусть так. По небесам
я курс не проложу меж звезд и капель.
Пусть эхо тут разносит по лесам
не песнь, а кашель.

10

Сентябрь. Ночь. Всё общество — свеча.
Но тень еще глядит из-за плеча
в мои листы и роется в корнях
оборванных. И призрак твой в сенях
шуршит и булькает водою
и улыбается звездою
в распахнутых рывком дверях.

11

The light fades out above my head.
The water covers up my tracks.
My heart rushes toward you—
harder and harder, farther and farther.
A falser and falser note creeps into my voice.
But you will set this down to fate,
a fate which does not ask for blood
but wounds me with a blunted needle.
And if you're hoping for a smile—
just wait, I'll smile! My smile will float
above me like the grave's long-standing
roof, lighter than woodsmoke.

Euterpe, is it you? Where am I?
What's this beneath me: water, grass,
the offshoot of a heather lyre,
curved to a horseshoe shape
that seems to promise luck—
a shape that neither you nor your
Calliope can know, moving
at quickened pace, full gallop, fast enough
to take your breath away.

11

Темнеет надо мною свет.
Вода затягивает след.
Да, сердце рвется всё сильней к тебе,
и оттого оно — всё дальше.
И в голосе моем всё больше фальши.
Но ты ее сочти за долг судьбе,
за долг судьбе, не требующей крови
и ранящей иглой тупой.
А если ты улыбку ждешь — постой!
Я улыбнусь. Улыбка над собой
могильной долговечней кровли
и легче дыма над печной трубой.

12

Эвтерпа, ты? Куда зашел я, а?
И что здесь подо мной: вода, трава,
отросток лиры вересковой,
изогнутый такой подковой,
что счастье чудится,
такой, что, может быть,
как перейти на иноходь с галопа
так быстро и дыхания не сбить,
не ведаешь ни ты, ни Каллиопа.

VERSES ON THE DEATH OF T. S. ELIOT

I

He died at start of year, in January.
His front door flinched in frost by the streetlamp.
There was no time for nature to display
the splendours of her choreography.
Black windowpanes shrank mutely in the snow.
The cold's town-crier stood beneath the light.
At crossings puddles stiffened into ice.
He latched his door on the thin chain of years.

The Muses' Holy Family will not brand
his gift of days a bankrupt. Poetry
is orphaned, yet it breeds within the glass
of lonely days, each echoing each, that swim
to distance. It will splash against the eye,
sink into lymph, like some Aeolian nymph,
a narcissistic friend. But in the rhyme
of years the voice of poetry stands plain.

With neither grimace nor maliciousness
death chooses from its bulging catalogue
the poet, not his words, however strong,
but just—unfailingly—the poet's self.
It has no use for thickets or for fields
or seas in their high, bright magnificence,
Death is a prodigal, it piles
a horde of hearts upon a wisp of time.

Used Christmas trees had flared in vacant lots,
and broken baubles had been broomed away.
Winged angels nested warmly on their shelves.
A Catholic, he lived till Christmas Day.
But, as the sea, whose tide has climbed and roared,
slamming the seawall, draws its warring waves
down and away, so he, in haste, withdrew
from his own high and solemn victory.

СТИХИ НА СМЕРТЬ Т. С. ЭЛИОТА

I

Он умер в январе, в начале года.
Под фонарем стоял мороз у входа.
Не успевала показать природа
ему своих красот кордебалет.
От снега стекла становились уже.
Под фонарем стоял глашатай стужи.
На перекрестках замерзали лужи.
И дверь он запер на цепочку лет.

Наследство дней не упрекнет в банкротстве
семейство Муз. При всем своем сиротстве,
поэзия основана на сходстве
бегущих вдаль однообразных дней.
Плеснув в зрачке и растворившись в лимфе,
она сродни лишь эолийской нимфе,
как друг Нарцисс. Но в календарной рифме
она другим наверняка видней.

Без злых гримас, без помышленья злого,
из всех щедрот Большого Каталога
смерть выбирает не красоты слога,
а неизменно самого певца.
Ей не нужны поля и перелески,
моря во всем великолепном блеске.
Она щедра, на небольшом отрезке
себе позволив накоплять сердца.

На пустырях уже пылали елки,
и выметались за порог осколки,
и водворялись ангелы на полке.
Католик, он дожил до Рождества.
Но, словно море в шумный час прилива,
за волнолом плеснувши, справедливо
назад вбирает волны — торопливо
от своего ушел он торжества.

It was not God, but only time, mere time
that called him. The young tribe of giant waves
will bear the burden of his flight until
it strikes the far edge of its flowering fringe,
to bid a slow farewell, breaking against
the limit of the earth. Exuberant
in strength, it laughs, a January gulf
in that dry land of days where we remain.

II

Where are you, Magi, you who read men's souls?
Come now and hold his halo high for him.
Two mournful figures gaze upon the ground.
They sing. How very similar their songs!
Are they then maidens? One cannot be sure:
pain and not passion has defined their sex.
One seems an Adam, turning half away,
but, judging by his flow of hair, an Eve . . .

America, where he was born and raised,
and England, where he died—they both incline
their drowsy faces as they stand, dejectedly,
on either side of his enormous grave.
And ships of cloud swim slowly heavenward.

But each grave is the limit of the earth.

III

Apollo, fling your garland down.
Let it be the poet's crown,
sign of immortality,
all there is where mortals be.

Forests here will not forget
voice of lyre and rush of feet.
Only what remains alive
will deserve their memories.

Уже не Бог, а только время, Время
зовет его. И молодое племя
огромных волн его движенья бремя
на самый край цветущей бахромы
легко возносит и, простившись, бьется
о край земли. В избытке сил смеется.
И январем его залив вдается
в ту сушу дней, где остаемся мы.

II

Читающие в лицах, маги, где вы?
Сюда! И поддержите ореол:
Две скорбные фигуры смотрят в пол.
Они поют. Как схожи их напевы!
Две девы — и нельзя сказать, что девы:
не страсть, а боль определяет пол.
Одна похожа на Адама впол-
оборота. Но прическа — Евы...

Склоняя лица сонные свои,
Америка, где он родился, и,
и Англия, где умер он, унылы,
стоят по сторонам его могилы.
И туч плывут по небу корабли.

Но каждая могила — край земли.

III

Аполлон, сними венок.
Положи его у ног
Элиота, как предел
для бессмертья в мире тел.

Шум шагов и лиры звук
будет помнить лес вокруг.
Будет памяти служить
только то, что будет жить.

Hill and dale will not forget.
Aeolus will know him yet.
Blades of grass his memory hold,
just as Horace had foretold.

Thomas Stearns, don't dread the sheep,
or the reaper's deadly sweep.
If you're not recalled by stone,
puffball drift will make you known.

Thus it is that love takes flight.
Once for all. Into the night.
Cutting through all words and cries,
seen no more, and yet alive.

You have gone where others are.
We, in envy of your star,
call that vast and hidden room,
thoughtlessly, "the realm of gloom".

Wood and field will not forget.
All that lives will know him yet—
as the body keeps alive
lost caress of lips and eyes.

Будет помнить лес и дол.
Будет помнить сам Эол.
Будет помнить каждый злак,
как хотел Гораций Флакк.

Томас Стернс, не бойся коз!
Безопасен сенокос.
Память — если не гранит —
одуванчик сохранит.

Так любовь уходит прочь.
Навсегда. В чужую ночь.
Прерывая крик, слова.
Став незримой, хоть жива.

Ты ушел к другим. Но мы
называем царством тьмы
этот край, который скрыт.
Это ревность так велит!

Будет помнить лес и луг.
Будет помнить всё вокруг.
Словно тело — мир не пуст! —
помнит ласку рук и уст.

THE FOUNTAIN

From the lion's jaws
no stream ripples, no roar sounds.
Hyacinths bloom. There is no whistle, no cry,
no voice at all. The leaves are motionless.
This is a strange setting for so threatening a visage,
a new setting.
His lips are parched,
his throat has rusted through; metal is not deathless.
The faucet has been turned completely off,
the faucet hidden among paradise trees near the end of his tail.
A nettle has clogged the valve. Evening descends;
from among the shrubs
a swarm of shadows
runs headlong toward the fountain, like lions from a thicket.
They crowd around their kinsman, who lies sleeping in the basin's
centre.
They leap over the edge and begin to float in the basin,
licking their leader's snout and paws. The more they lick,
the darker
grows his threatening visage.
Finally he mingles with them,
springs abruptly to life, leaps down; and the entire company
runs swiftly into the dark. The sky
hides its stars behind a cloud. Sober thinkers
call this
the abduction of the leader—
and, since the first drops are sparkling on the park bench,
they call this abduction of the leader a coming of rain.
The rain slopes its yardsticks toward the earth,
building a net or a cage, high in the air, for a lion's family,
using neither knots nor nails.
There is a
drizzle of
warm rain.
No chill touches the throats of the shadows,

ФОНТАН

Из пасти льва
струя не журчит и не слышно рыка.
Гиацинты цветут. Ни свистка, ни крика,
никаких голосов. Неподвижна листва.
И чужда обстановка сия для столь грозного лика,
и нова.
Пересохли уста,
и гортань проржавела: металл не вечен.
Просто кем-нибудь наглухо кран заверчен,
хоронящийся в кущах, в конце хвоста,
и крапива опутала вентиль. Спускается вечер;
из куста
сонм теней
выбегает к фонтану, как львы из чащи.
Окружают сородича, спящего в центре чаши,
перепрыгнув барьер, начинают носиться в ней,
лижут морду и лапы вождя своего. И, чем чаще,
тем темней
грозный облик. И вот
наконец он сливается с ними и резко
оживает и прыгает вниз. И всё общество резво
убегает во тьму. Небосвод
прячет звезды за тучу, и мыслящий трезво
назовет
похищенье вождя —
так как первые капли блестят на скамейке —
назовет похищенье вождя приближеньем дождя.
Дождь спускает на землю косые линейки,
строя в воздухе сеть или клетку для львиной семейки
без узла и гвоздя.
Теплый
дождь
моросит.
Но, как льву, им гортань
не остудишь.

or the lion's throat.
You will be neither loved nor forgotten.
And, if you were a monster, a company of monsters
will resurrect you, at a late hour, out of the earth.
Rain and snow
will proclaim
your triumph.
Not being subject to chest-colds,
you will return to this world to spend the night.
No loneliness is deeper than the memory of miracles.
Former inmates return to their prisons;
doves return to the Ark.

Ты не будешь любим и забыт не будешь.

И тебя в поздний час из земли воскресит,

если чудищем был ты, компания чудищ.

Разгласит

твой побег

дождь и снег.

И, не склонный к простуде,

всё равно ты вернешься в сей мир на ночлег.

Ибо нет одиночества больше, чем память о чуде.

Так в тюрьму возвращаются в ней побывавшие люди

и голубки — в ковчег.

V The Dioscuri—Castor and Pollux—were, in Greek mythology, a symbol
of indissoluble friendship. Their image was used on Greek coins. Greeks
of the classical period considered it blasphemous to depict rulers on coins;
they depicted only gods, their symbols, or mythological personages.

VI Lemnos: an island in the Aegean Sea which served, and still serves, as a
place of exile.

X A pun in the original Russian: *Verzuvii* ("Versuvius") rather than *Vezuvii*
("Vesuvius"), suggesting the Church Slavonic *verzati*, "to open or gape".

XII *Thalatta*: Greek for "sea".

POST AETATEM NOSTRAM

To Andrei Sergeyev

I

"The Empire is a country for dull fools."
All traffic has been stopped in preparation
for the Emperor's arrival. A dense crowd
washes against the Legionnaires. Singing
and shouts. The curtains of a palanquin
are drawn; love's object shuns all curious glances.

In a deserted coffee-shop behind
the palace a vagrant Greek plays dominoes
with an unshaven crippled veteran.
Parings of light tossed from the street criss-cross
the tablecloths; faint echoes of festivity
flutter the shades. The victorious Greek counts up
his drachmas, then he bids them bring a pinch
of salt and hard-boiled eggs.

In a high-ceilinged bedchamber an old
state-merchant tells a young hetaera how
he saw the Emperor. Incredulous,

ПРИМЕЧАНИЯ

Перевод заглавия: ПОСЛЕ НАШЕЙ ЭРЫ

V — Диоскуры: Кастор и Поллукс (Кастор и Полидевк), в греческой мифологии символ нерасторжимой дружбы. Их изображение помещалось на греческих монетах. Греки классического периода считали богохульством изображения государей; изображались только боги или их символы; также — мифологические персонажи.

VI — Лемнос: остров в Эгейском море, служил и служит местом ссылки.

X — Верзувий: от славянского «верзати.»

XII — Таллатта: греч. «море».

Андрею Сергееву

I

«Империя — страна для дураков.»
Движенье перекрыто по причине
приезда Императора. Толпа
теснит легионеров, песни, крики;
но паланкин закрыт. Объект любви
не хочет быть объектом любопытства.

В пустой кофейне позади дворца
бродяга-грек с небритым инвалидом
играют в домино. На скатертях
лежат отбросы уличного света,
и отголоски likованья мирно
шевелят шторы. Проигравший грек
считает драхмы; победитель просит
яйцо вкрутую и щепотку соли.

В просторной спальне старый откупщик
рассказывает молодой гетере,
что видел Императора. Гетера

271

she laughs aloud. Such is the prelude to
their game of love.

II

The Palace

A satyr and a nymph, immobilized
in marble, gaze into the pool's clear depths;
its mirror-surface glows with rose-petals.

The bare-foot Governor, with his own fists,
bloodies the soft nose of the local King
because of the three pigeons baked in dough
(when the meat-pie was sliced, they all flew out
but quickly fell like stones on the great table).
The King's banquet—perhaps his life—is ruined.

The King writhes silently on the wet floor,
pinned by the Governor's tough, sinewy knee.
Rose-fragrance fogs the walls. The servants stare,
like statues, straight ahead, betraying not
the least flicker of interest. Polished stones
give back no clear reflection of the deed.

By the unsteady light of the Northern moon
the vagrant Greek, curled up beside the chimney
in the palace kitchen, strokes a cat
and watches as two slaves bring out the cook's
limp body, loosely wrapped in net, and slowly
make their way down to the river. The gravel
underfoot emits a crunching sound.

A man perched on the roof clamps shut a cat-mouth.

III

A barber whose boy helper has just left him
stares silently at his mirror-reflection;
distraught at the boy's absence, he forgets

не верит и хохочет. Таковы
прелюдии у них к любовным играм.

II

Дворец

Изваянные в мраморе сатир
и нимфа смотрят в глубину бассейна,
чья гладь покрыта лепестками роз.

Наместник, босиком, собственноручно
кровавит морду местному царю
за трех голубок, угоревших в тесте
(в момент разделки пирога взлетевших
но тотчас же попадавших на стол).
Испорчен праздник, если не карьера.

Царь молча извивается на мокром
полу под мощным, жилистым коленом
Наместника. Благоуханье роз
туманит стены. Слуги безучастно
глядят перед собой, как изваянья.
Но в гладком камне отраженья нет.
В неверном свете северной луны,
свернувшись у трубы дворцовой кухни,
бродяга-грек в обнимку с кошкой смотрят,
как два раба выносят из дверей
труп повара, завернутый в рогожу,
и медленно спускаются к реке.
Шуршит щебенка.
               Человек на крыше
старается зажать кошачью пасть.

III

Покинутый мальчишкой брадобрей
глядится молча в зеркало — должно быть,
грустя о нем и начисто забыв

the lathered face of his lone customer.
"I don't suppose he will come back again."

Meantime, the customer is calmly dozing,
dreaming Greek dreams—of gods, cithara-players,
athletic contests in gymnasiums where the
sharp smell of sweat tickles the nostrils.
                                    Swooping
down from the ceiling, a huge housefly circles
the room and, landing on the sleeper's cheek,
sinks into the white lather, like those poor
peltasts (in Xenophon) into the snowdrifts
of Armenia, and slowly crawls,
past ledges and ravines, up toward the summit,
avoids the crater-mouth, and manages
to gain the very tip of the Greek's nose.

The Greek opens his terrible black eye;
the fly, abuzz with horror, darts away.

IV

After wet holidays the night is dry.
Like a starved horse, the flapping flag at the gate
grinds wind between its jagged teeth. The labyrinthine, empty streets are bathed in moonlight;
the prisoned monster must be sound asleep.

The farther out one goes from the great palace
the fewer are the statues and bright pools.
Stuccoed façades are rare. And every door
that opens on a balcony is closed.
Walls are the lone night-guardians of men's peace.

The sound of one's own footsteps is both ominous
and vulnerable. Fish smells pervade the air.
The houses now have all been left behind.

намыленную голову клиента.
«Наверно, мальчик больше не вернется.»

Тем временем клиент спокойно дремлет
и видит чисто греческие сны:
с богами, с кифаредами, с борьбой
в гимназиях, где острый запах пота
щекочет ноздри.
                    Снявшись с потолка,
большая муха, сделав круг, садится
на белую намыленную щеку
заснувшего и, утопая в пене
как бедные пельтасты Ксенофонта
в снегах армянских, медленно ползет
через провалы, выступы, ущелья
к вершине и, минуя жерло рта,
взобраться норовит на кончик носа.

Грек открывает страшный черный глаз,
и муха, взвыв от ужаса, взлетает.

IV
Сухая послепраздничная ночь.
Флаг в подворотне, схожий с конской мордой,
жует губами воздух. Лабиринт
пустынных улиц залит лунным светом;
чудовище, должно быть, крепко спит.

Чем дальше от дворца, тем меньше статуй
и луж. С фасадов исчезает лепка.
И если дверь выходит на балкон,
она закрыта. Видимо и здесь
ночной покой спасают только стены.

Звук собственных шагов вполне зловещ
и в то же время беззащитен; воздух
уже пронизан рыбою: дома

But the moon-rippled road keeps flowing on.
A black felucca prowls across it, cat-like,
dissolving in the dark, to let us know
that, really, there's no sense in venturing
beyond this point.

V

In a "Message to the Rulers" which is posted
on every street-billboard a well-known local
bard, seething with indignation,
calls boldly for removal of the Imperial
likeness (in the line that follows next)
from every copper coin.

The crowd is animated. Youths, grey-haired
old men, men in their prime, and literate
hetaeras are all agreed on this:
"There never has been such a thing before."
They don't, however, make it clear what sort
of thing they have in mind; do they mean "courage,"
or merely "loutishness"?

No doubt it is the mark of poetry
to draw no sharp frontier between the two.

A sea-horizon, blue beyond belief.
Breakers that roar and hiss. A naked man,
stretched full-length on a dry and burning rock
like some lizard in March, snaps off the shells
of stolen almonds. Far away two slaves,
chained hard together, clumsily assist
each other as they shed their tattered clothes,
preparing for an ocean bath. They laugh
aloud.
        The day is hot beyond belief.

кончаются.
                    Но лунная дорога
струится дальше. Черная фелукка
ее пересекает, словно кошка,
и растворяется во тьме, дав знак,
что дальше, собственно, идти не стоит.

                         V
В расклеенном на уличных щитах
«Послании к властителям» известный,
известный местный кифаред, кипя
негодованьем, смело выступает
с призывом Императора убрать
(на следующей строчке) с медных денег.

Толпа жестикулирует. Юнцы,
седые старцы, зрелые мужчины
и знающие грамоте гетеры
единогласно утверждают, что
«такого прежде не было» — при этом
не уточняя, именно чего
«такого»:
                    мужества или холуйства.

Поэзия, должно быть, состоит
в отсутствии отчетливой границы.

Невероятно синий горизонт.
Шуршание прибоя. Растянувшись,
как ящерица в марте, на сухом
горячем камне, голый человек
лущит ворованный миндаль. Поодаль
два скованных между собой раба,
собравшиеся, видно, искупаться,
смеясь друг другу помогают снять
свое тряпье.
                    Невероятно жарко;

The Greek slips down from the flat rock, his eyes
like two bright silver drachmas, imaging
a new pair of Dioscuri.

VI

The acoustics here are faultless! Not in vain
was the architect a feast for Lemnian lice
during seventeen long years. Superb acoustics!

The day, too, is delightful. And the crowd,
having poured itself into a stadium-shape,
freezes and holds its breath, as it drinks in
the abuse which the two fighters in the arena
heap on each other to inflame their tempers;
then they draw their swords.

The purpose of the fight is not mere killing,
but death that is both just and logical.
The laws of drama are transferred to sport.

The acoustics are superb. The stands are filled
with men, no women. Sunlight turns to gold
the tousled lions on the royal box.
The stadium has become one giant ear.

"You rotten carrion!" "Carrion! So are you!"
"Mere trash and carrion!" Now the Governor,
his face a festering udder, laughs aloud.

VII

The Tower

The midday air is cool.
The iron spires of the city Tower; its tip
lost in the clouds, serves as a lightning-rod,
a lighthouse, and a flagpole for the flag
of state. Inside, it holds a prison.

и грек сползает с камня, закатив
глаза, как две серебрянные драхмы
с изображеньем новых Диоскуров.

VI

Прекрасная акустика! Строитель
недаром вшей кормил семнадцать лет
на Лемносе. Акустика прекрасна.
День тоже восхитителен. Толпа,
отлившаяся в форму стадиона,
застыв и затаив дыханье, внемлет
той ругани, которой два бойца
друг друга осыпают на арене,
чтоб, распалясь, схватиться за мечи.

Цель состязанья вовсе не в убийстве,
но в справедливой и логичной смерти.
Законы драмы переходят в спорт.

Акустика прекрасна. На трибунах
одни мужчины. Солнце золотит
кудлатых львов правительственной ложи.
Весь стадион — одно большое ухо.

«Ты падаль!» «Сам ты падаль». «Мразь и падаль!»
И тут Наместник, чье лицо подобно
гноящемуся вымени, смеется.

VII

Башня

Прохладный полдень.
Теряющийся где-то в облаках
железный шпиль муниципальной башни
является в одно и то же время
громоотводом, маяком и местом
подъема государственного флага.
Внутри же — размещается тюрьма

As a rough rule, it has been estimated—
in Persian satrapies, under the Pharaohs,
in Islam, in the Christian epoch too—
that six percent of the whole population
has suffered either death or life in prison.
For this reason, a century ago
the grandsire of the present Emperor
conceived a project of legal reform.
By a special decree he put an end
to the death penalty, an evil thing;
reduced from six percent to only two
the number of those doomed to spend their lives
in jail. The law was like a tax; it did
not differentiate between those persons
guilty in fact of crimes and the innocent.
It was then that the city Tower was built.
A blinding flash of chromium-plated steel.
A shepherd, on the Tower's forty-third floor,
his head thrust through a porthole, sends a smile
of welcome to the sheepdog which has come
to visit him.

VIII

The fountain, which depicts a porpoise leaping
in the open sea, is now entirely dry.
That's understandable: a marble fish
has no serious need for water, any more
than marble water has a need for fish.

This is a court-of-arbitration verdict,
noted—like all such verdicts—for its dryness.
On the wide marble steps that lead up to
the white columns of the palace, a small group
of dark-skinned local chiefs in gaudy, crumpled
robes awaits the appearance of their King—
like scattered flowers on a white tablecloth,
flung from a water-filled glass vase.

Подсчитано когда-то, что обычно —
в сатрапиях, во время фараонов,
у мусульман, в эпоху христианства —
сидело иль бывало казнено
примерно шесть процента населенья.
Поэтому еще сто лет назад
дед нынешнего цезаря задумал
реформу правосудия. Отменив
безнравственный обычай смертной казни,
он с помощью особого закона
те шесть процента сократил до двух,
обязанных сидеть в тюрьме, конечно,
пожизненно. Неважно, совершил ли
ты преступленье или невиновен;
закон, по сути дела, как налог.
Тогда-то и воздвигли эту Башню.
Слепящий блеск хромированной стали.
На сорок третьем этаже пастух,
лицо просунув сквозь иллюминатор,
свою улыбку посылает вниз
пришедшей навестить его собаке.

VIII

Фонтан, изображающий дельфина
в открытом море, совершенно сух.
Вполне понятно: каменная рыба
способна обойтись и без воды,
как та — без рыбы, сделанной из камня.

Таков вердикт третейского суда.
Чьи приговоры отличает сухость.

Под белой колоннадою дворца
на мраморных ступеньках кучка смуглых
вождей в измятых пестрых балахонах
ждет появленья своего царя,

как брошенный на скатерти букет —
заполненной водой стеклянной вазы.

The King appears. The chiefs stand up and shake
their lances. Kisses, hugs, and smiles. The King is
embarrassed; but dark skin has this advantage:
when bruised, it does not show its black-and-blueness.

The vagrant Greek summons a boy to him.
"What are they chattering about?" "Who, them?"
"Uh-huh." "They're thanking him." "For what?" The boy
raises his lucid eyes: "For laying down
new laws against the poor."

IX

The Caged Beast
The heavy bars which block the lion off
from curious men are an iron variant
on jungle thickets.

Green moss. Drops of metallic dew. A lotus
wrapped in thin lianas.

Here nature is mimicked with special love,
the kind which only men can bring to bear,
since only they can see the difference
between going astray in matted jungles
and getting lost in empty wilderness.

X

The Emperor
A burly Legionnaire in gleaming armour,
now standing guard beside the high white door
(a gurgling sound can just be heard behind it),
stares through a window at the lovely women.
It seems to him—he has stood for an hour—
that there is only one woman inside,
not many.

Царь появляется. Вожди встают
и потрясают копьями. Улыбки,
объятья, поцелуи. Царь слегка
смущен; но вот удобство смуглой кожи:
на ней не так видны кровоподтеки.

Бродяга-грек зовет к себе мальца.
«О чем они болтают?» «Кто, вот эти?»
«Ага.» «Благодарят его.» «За что?»
Мальчишка поднимает ясный взгляд:
«За новые законы против нищих.»

IX

Зверинец

Решетка, отделяющая льва
от публики, в чугунном варианте
воспроизводит путаницу джунглей.

Мох. Капли металлической росы.
Лиана, оплетающая лотос.

Природа имитируется с той
любовью, на которую способен
лишь человек, которому не все
равно, где заблудиться: в чаще или
в пустыне.

X

Император

Атлет-легионер в блестящих латах,
несущий стражу возле белой двери,
из-за которой слышится журчанье,
глядит в окно на проходящих женщин.
Ему, торчащему здесь битый час,
уже казаться начинает, будто
не разные красавицы внизу
проходят мимо, но одна и та же.

The large gold letter "M" which decorates
the door seems small compared to that huge one
which, flushed with the exertion, crouches down
behind the door in order to inspect
each least detail of its reflection in
the swiftly-flowing water.

When all is said and done, such flowing waters
are no worse than the sculptors who have flooded
the Empire with this image.

A clear and gurgling stream. An upside-down
Vesuvius hangs huge above it, slow
to start erupting.
It seems that everything runs creakingly.
The Empire's like a trireme in a tight
canal too narrow for its hull. The rowers
bang their oars on the dry land; sharp stones
scrape hard against the planks. No, do not say
that we have run aground! We're still afloat
and moving; yes, we're under way. And no
one overtakes us. Yet, alas, how stark
the contrast with our past Imperial speed!
And how can anyone fail to sigh for
those times, long past, when everything went smoothly,
and almost without hitch.

XI

A lamp goes out; its wick is smouldering
in the dark room. A thin ribbon of smoke
curls toward the ceiling; at first glance, its whiteness,
in that unleavened darkness, is commensurate
with any form of light. Even soot.
                                     Outside
the window all night long an Asian rainstorm

Большая золотая буква М,
украсившая дверь, по сути дела
лишь прописная по сравненью с той,
огромной и пунцовой от натуги,
согнувшейся за дверью над проточной
водою, дабы рассмотреть во всех
подробностях свое отображенье.

В конце концов, проточная вода
ничуть не хуже скульпторов, все царство
изображеньем этим наводнивших.

Прозрачная, журчащая струя.
Огромный, перевернутый Верзувий,
над ней нависнув, медлит с изверженьем.

Все вообще теперь идет со скрипом.
Империя похожа на трирему
в канале, для триремы слишком узком.
Гребцы колотят веслами по суше,
и камни сильно обдирают борт.
Нет, не сказать, чтоб мы совсем застряли!
Движенье есть, движенье происходит.
Мы все-таки плывем. И нас никто
пс обгоняет. Но, увы, как мало
похоже это на былую скорость!
И как тут не вздохнуть о временах,
когда все шло довольно гладко.

                              Гладко.

XI

Светильник гаснет, и фитиль чадит
уже в потемках. Тоненькая струйка
всплывает к потолку, чья белизна
в кромешном мраке в первую минуту
согласна на любую форму света.
Пусть даже копоть.

                    За окном всю ночь
в неполотом саду шумит тяжелый

roars in the unweeded garden. But the mind
stays dry. So dry that, when it is embraced
by the cold, pallid flame of love, it bursts
into a riotous blaze faster even than
thinnest paper or driest brushwood.

The ceiling does not see this blinding flash.

A man, leaving behind him neither soot
nor ashes, wades into the dripping darkness
and wanders toward the wicket-gate. The silver
voice of a chimney-swift summons him back.

In heavy rain he obediently returns
to the great kitchen and, unfastening
his belt, pours the remaining drachmas out
on the iron table. Then he leaves for good.
The bird is silent.

XII

Having decided to recross the border,
the Greek got a large sack and, in the square
near the main market, filled it up with cats—
twelve cats, all black. With this meowing, scratch-
ing load he came at night to a dense forest
near the border.

The moon was shining, as it always shines
in mid-July. Of course the watchdogs poured
their mournful howls throughout the great ravine.
The cats stopped squabbling in the sack and nearly
fell silent. Then the Greek spoke quietly:
"May my luck hold. Athena, do thou not
abandon me. Walk thou before me." To
himself he added: "I shall use six cats
here at this stretch of the frontier—no more."

азийский ливень. Но рассудок — сух.
Настолько сух, что, будучи охвачен
холодным бледным пламенем объятья,
воспламеняешься быстрей, чем лист
бумаги или старый хворост.

Но потолок не видит этой вспышки.

Ни копоти, ни пепла по себе
не оставляя, человек выходит
в сырую темень и бредет к калитке.
Но серебристый голос козодоя
велит ему вернуться.

          Под дождем
он, повинуясь, снова входит в кухню
и, снявши пояс, высыпает на
железный стол оставшиеся драхмы.
Затем выходит.
Птица не кричит.

XII

Задумав перейти границу, грек
достал вместительный мешок и после
в кварталах возле рынка изловил
двенадцать кошек (почерней) и с этим
скребущимся, мяукающим грузом
он прибыл ночью в пограничный лес.

Луна светила, как она всегда
в июле светит. Псы сторожевые
конечно заливали все ущелье
тоскливым лаем: кошки перестали
в мешке скандалить и почти притихли.
И грек промолвил тихо: «В добрый час.

Афина, не оставь меня. Ступай
передо мной.» — а про себя добавил:
«На эту часть границы я кладу
всего шесть кошек. Ни одною больше.»

The watchdogs will not venture to the pinewoods.
As for the soldiers—they are superstitious.

It all worked out in the best way conceivable.
The moon, the dogs, the cats, the superstition,
and the pinetrees—the whole system functioned
perfectly. He gained the high divide.
But at the very moment when he stood,
one foot across the border, he discovered
the thing he had forgotten.
                                    Turning round,
he caught sight of the sea.

It lay beneath him, far away. Now men,
in contrast to the other animals,
are capable of leaving what they love
(if only to prove that they are not beasts).
His tears, like dog's saliva, gave away
the secret of his animality.
"O, Thalatta!"
                        But in this sinful world
one must not stand, in moonlight, on a high
divide, unless one wants to be a target.
Heaving the sack up onto his back, the Greek
began his slow descent into the depths
of the great continent.
                              What rose to meet him
was a crest of pines, not sea-horizon.

Собака не взберется на сосну.
Что до солдат — солдаты суеверны.

Все вышло лучшим образом. Луна,
собаки, кошки, суеверье, сосны —
весь механизм сработал. Он взобрался
на перевал. Но в миг, когда уже
одной ногой стоял в другой державе,
он обнаружил то, что упустил:
оборотившись, он увидел море.

Оно лежало далеко внизу.
В отличье от животных, человек
уйти способен от того, что любит
(чтоб только отличиться от животных!).
Но, как слюна собачья, выдают
его животную природу слезы:

«О, Талатта!..»
                    Но в этом скверном мире
нельзя торчать так долго на виду,
на перевале, в лунном свете, если
не хочешь стать мишенью. Вскинув ношу,
он осторожно стал спускаться вниз,
вглубь континента; и вставал навстречу

еловый гребень вместо горизонта.

NATURE MORTE

Verrà la morte e avrà i tuoi occhi.
C. Pavese

1

People and things crowd in.
My eyes are bruised and hurt
by people as well as things.
Better to live in dark.

I sit on a wooden bench
watching the passers-by—
sometimes whole families.
I am fed up with light.

This is a winter month,
first on the calendar.
I shall begin to speak
when I'm fed up with dark.

2

It's time. I shall now begin.
It makes no difference with what.
Open mouth. It is better to speak,
though I can also be mute.

What shall I talk about?
The nothing that fills our lives.
About days, about nights. About things,
not people, but only things,

since people will surely die.
And I too shall die, like them.
All talk is a barren trade,
like writing upon the wind.

НАТЮРМОРТ

Verrà la morte e avrà i tuoi occhi.
C. Pavese

I

Вещи и люди нас
окружают. И те,
и эти терзают глаз.
Лучше жить в темноте.

Я сижу на скамье
в парке, глядя вослед
проходящей семье.
Мне опротивел свет.

Это январь. Зима.
Согласно календарю.
Когда опротивеет тьма,
тогда я заговорю.

2

Пора. Я готов начать.
Неважно, с чего. Открыть
рот. Я могу молчать.
Но лучше мне говорить.

О чём? О днях, о ночах.
Или же — ничего.
Или же о вещах.
О вещах, а не о

людях. Они умрут.
Все. Я тоже умру.
Это бесплодный труд.
Как писать на ветру.

3

My blood is very cold—
its cold is more withering
than iced-to-the-bottom streams.
People are not my thing.

I hate the look of them.
Grafted to life's great tree,
each face is glued and fixed,
never to be wrenched free.

Something the mind abhors
shows in each face and form.
Something like flattery
of someone quite unknown.

4

Things are much pleasanter.
Their surfaces, though not good,
aren't evil. And one who looks
within them, finds insides too.

At the centre of things—dry rot.
Partitions, moth-wings, and dust.
Dead ashes and wood-borers.
Strange to the finger's touch.

Dust. When you switch lights on,
there's nothing but dust to see.
That's true even if the thing
is sealed up hermetically.

5

This ancient chest-of-drawers—
inside and out: the same—
strangely reminds me of
Paris's Notre Dame.

3

Кровь моя холодна.
Холод ее лютей
реки, промерзшей до дна.
Я не люблю людей.

Внешность их не по мне.
Лицами их привит
к жизни какой-то не-
покидаемый вид.

Что-то в их лицах есть,
что противно уму.
Что выражает лесть
неизвестно кому.

4

Вещи приятней. В них
нет ни зла, ни добра
внешне. А если вник
в них — и внутри нутра.

Внутри у предметов — пыль.
Прах. Древоточец-жук.
Стенки. Сухой мотыль.
Неудобно для рук.

Пыль. И включенный свет
только пыль озарит.
Даже если предмет
герметично закрыт.

5

Старый буфет извне
так же, как изнутри,
напоминает мне
Нотр-Дам де Пари.

Everything's dark within
it. Dustmop and bishop's stole
can't touch the dust of things.
Things themselves, as a rule,

don't try to purge or tame
the dust of their own insides.
Dust is the flesh of time,
time's very flesh and blood.

6

Lately I often sleep
during the daytime. My
death, it would seem, is now
trying and testing me,

looking-glass at my lips,
even though I still breathe,
seeing if I can stand
non-being in daylight.

I do not move. My thighs
are like two icicles.
The blueness of my veins
has a cold-marble look.

7

Summing their angles up
as a surprise to us,
things drop away from man's
world—a world made with words.

Things do not move or stand.
That's our delirium.
Each thing's a space, beyond
which there can be no thing.

В недрах буфета тьма.
Швабра, епитрахиль
пыль не сотрут. Сама
вещь, как правило, пыль

не тщится перебороть,
не напрягает бровь.
Ибо пыль — это плоть
времени; плоть и кровь.

6

Последнее время я
сплю среди бела дня.
Видимо, смерть моя
испытывает меня,

поднося, хоть дышу,
зеркало мне ко рту, —
как я переношу
небытие на свету.

Я неподвижен. Два
бедра холодны, как лёд.
Венозная синева
мрамором отдаёт.

7

Преподнося сюрприз
суммой своих углов,
вещь выпадает из
нашего мира слов.

Вещь не стоит. И не
движется. Это — бред.
Вещь есть пространство, вне
коего вещи нет.

Things are slammed down, and burned,
gutted, and broken up.
Thrown out. Despite all this,
things never yell, "O, fuck!"

8

A tree. Its shadow, and
earth, pierced by probing roots—
interlaced monograms.
Clay and a clutch of rocks.

Roots interweave and blend.
Boulders have their own mass
which frees them from the bond
of normal rootedness.

Boulders are fixed. One can't
move them, or heave them out.
Shadows have caught a man
like a fish in their net.

9

Things. Their brown colour, their
blurry outlines. Twilight.
Now there is nothing left.
Only a *nature morte*.

Death comes and finds a corpse
whose surface, mirror-like,
will reflect death's approach
like closeness of a wife.

Scythe, skull, and skeleton—
an absurd pack of lies.
"Death, when it comes, will be
like you and have your eyes."

Вещь можно грохнуть, сжечь,
распотрошить, сломать.
Бросить. При этом вещь
не крикнет: «Ебёна мать!»

                    8
Дерево. Тень. Земля.
Под деревом уз корней
цепкие вензеля.
Глина. Гряда камней.

Корни. Их переплёт.
Камень, чей личный груз
освобождает от
данной системы уз.

Он неподвижен. Ни
сдвинуть, ни унести.
Тень. Человек в тени,
словно рыба в сети.

                    9
Вещь. Коричневый цвет
вещи. Чей контур стёрт.
Сумерки. Больше нет
ничего. Натюрморт.

Смерть придёт и найдёт
тело, чья гладь визит
смерти, точно приход
женщины, отразит.

Это абсурд, враньё:
череп, скелет, коса.
«Смерть придёт, у неё
будут твои глаза».

Christ's mother speaks to him:
"Art thou my God, or Son?
Thou art nailed to the cross.
How can I rest at home?

How can I find my way,
uncertain and afraid?
Art thou my dying son,
or my still living God?

Christ speaks to her in turn:
"Whether I live or die,
woman, it's all the same—
son or God, I am thine."

10

Мать говорит Христу:
— Ты мой сын или мой
Бог? Ты прибит к кресту.
Как я пойду домой?

Как ступлю на порог,
не узнав, не решив:
ты мой сын или Бог?
То есть, мёртв или жив? —

Он говорит в ответ:
— Мертвый или живой,
разницы, жено, нет.
Сын или Бог, я твой.

Constantine Constantinovich
Kuzminsky

Constantine Kuzminsky lives for poetry. A man possessed with a love for poetry and art so intense that it consumes him, he never stops talking about it, ignoring food, sleep, and time. His memory for poetry is extraordinary. When another poet forgets his own lines, Kuzminsky can pick them up without faltering. He attends every reading and has followed the development of modern Leningrad poetry for the past ten years with meticulous care and total devotion.

He knows every street and stone in his beloved Petersburg. He calls its architecture "crystallized music" and there is no building, no statue in Leningrad on which he cannot deliver an oration. He has absorbed the culture of two and a half centuries of the city's history and says with simple finality, "I cannot live without this view."

Like all who are possessed with absolute convictions, Kuzminsky is controversial. He is abrasive, exasperating even his closest friends. Single-minded devotion to an ideal of beauty is anachronistic in a twentieth-century world of machines and organization men. His way would be hard anywhere; in Russia it is especially so. Bitingly honest, combative and quick, he despises currying favours. "Even in school," he recalls, "I was beaten every day for my waspish tongue."

Because of his knowledge and his analytical mind, and perhaps even more because of the passion with which he lives and talks, he has been sought out for his ideas. He is theoretician, critic, guru and he has friends everywhere, high and low—poets, painters, musicians, dancers, engineers, sports heroes, workmen and scientists. He is constantly surrounded by them. They protect him, lend him money, worry about his health. They do not always understand him, and often disapprove of his behaviour, but they treat him with the special gentleness and understanding that Russians reserve for strange, mystic beings. *Bessrebrenik*, he has been called—a Russian expression meaning a person who is disinterested in worldly goods, who puts ideals higher than money.

He gives everything away, he never has any money in his pockets; his time belongs to everyone around him. Although highly critical, he has an unerring sense for what is beautiful and is quick to recognize and celebrate the talents of others. He listens to every poet who comes to him, he judges the work of every painter he knows. He encourages all of them, poets and painters alike, to do their best, goading them to strive for excellence. "To find art," he says, "it must be an individual search."

Every night this strange, passionate man wanders the city, walking along the canals and embankments whose minutest details he knows and loves. He visits everywhere in the city, drinking, talking, endlessly talking about poetry, staying up whole nights. He recites poetry to everyone, to taxi drivers (they thank him) and even sometimes to the militia when they have brought him in for drinking. With his flowing beard and hair, his tall, slender figure is unmistakable and on his rambling walks he is recognized and stopped on the street by acquaintances from every walk of life. He seems not so much to have been born as to have stepped from the pages of Dostoevsky.

Kuzminsky's life is a kind of synthesis of the modern experience of Leningrad. His father studied painting and design at the Academy in Leningrad, and graduated in 1934 as a gifted illustrator. But it was a time when all independent careers were crushed in the terror of the Stalin purges. Kuzminsky's mother became a teacher of mechanical drawing at the Mathematical Institute. Young Constantine was born on April 16, 1940, fourteen months before the German invasion. His father was a communications officer in the army. He fought for Leningrad and died of wounds in 1941. His mother struggled to raise her son through the Seige. Like thousands of children he suffered from scurvy, malnutrition and dystrophy. Today, although he is toughened and resilient from years of physical work, his health, like Sosnora's, suffers from the effects of those terrible years.

At the age of eight, Kuzminsky entered a school specializing in the English language. There he acquired a lasting love for English literature. He still speaks English well although he rarely has occasion to use the spoken language. Later, he studied biology at the University ("I loved snakes and serpents. I wanted to see South America and Africa. But instead, I read my way through the library and left to see Russia.") From 1960 to 1963, he worked as a jockey, a labourer, and a hydrologist on the Black Sea. He became a geological worker and went on geological expeditions to Siberia. Once, lost in the wilderness of the *taiga* during a great fire, he made his way, without a compass, 55 miles through the forest to find a village. His lungs were burned and he spent the winter recovering. It was during these months that he began to write his first poems.

In 1963, he returned to Leningrad and worked as a labourer in the Hermitage Museum. He was one of ten young men hired to shovel snow from the sidewalks in front of the museum and to clean the halls. Of these ten, eight were poets or painters and, inevitably, they formed groups for reading. In a room of the museum, the painters organized an art exhibition of their work, but after a single day, the authorities changed their minds and the exhibition was closed. At the time of Joseph Brodsky's trial, they wrote letters in his defence. Kuzminsky lost his job.

From 1963–7 he worked primarily as a guide (always for Russians, never for foreign tourists) in the magnificently restored Peterhof and Pavlovsk Palaces outside Leningrad. "There I polished my taste in art and architecture," he says. He knows every crystal bowl, every mahogany desk, every portrait in these great palaces. During this time he joined a poetry circle which met twice a week with Tatiana Gnedich, a prominent Leningrad teacher, poet and expert on Byron and the Victorian poets. Kuzminsky has worked as her literary secretary and began his Russian translations of Byron under her supervision. Tatiana Gnedich has called him "very gifted" and she has supported and criticized his work. He began to hold public readings of his own verses and his Byron translations in various libraries and lecture rooms.

His verses have been set to music; one of his very early short poems "Fog" became a popular hit and is often sung on the embankments of the Neva during the White Nights. Some of his poems have been broadcast on the radio, a few others in factory newspapers, and he was asked to write the text and poetic captions for a commemorative book on Leningrad to be published in Leningrad in English. During the past three years he has made his living by working as a summer guide in the Crimea in the famous Vorontsov Palace; for a brief time was caretaker at the Leningrad Zoo, and most recently has worked in a library.

With the exception of the Gnedich group, he has worked little with official poetry circles, preferring to work and to educate himself alone, reading whole nights through. Refusing to bow in any direction but the one he sees as his own, he always feels he knows better than any leader and falls into sharp theoretical discussions with them. While unofficial readings were still permitted, he was invited to read, but his loud and uncompromising arguments have driven away many who wished to help him.

Over the years, the strains of an intemperate life and the struggles and disappointments of the unofficial poet have taken a heavy toll. He is ill now, has spent many months in the hospital and undergone several serious operations. The clear mind and graceful accents of only a short time ago are now too often blurred by drink. Last year, while wandering the streets to admire a snowstorm he nearly froze to death and was saved only by the timely intervention of a young militiaman.

In the manner of romantic poets, Kuzminsky's private life has also been turbulent. (He has devoted much of his poetry to love—too much, his friends say.) He has been married four times. From his third marriage he has a beautiful daughter, now six years old. His wife is married again, but all are friendly, maintaining the kind of gregarious, understanding relationship Russians seem to manage uniquely well. He adores his child, visits her often and gently recites poetry to her until she goes to sleep.

He lives now with his ageing mother and his devoted wife Emma, a park architect, in a small apartment in the centre of old Petersburg, a few steps from the Neva and the famous Falconet statue of Peter the Great immortalized in Pushkin's *The Bronze Horseman*. Their apartment has about it a faintly archaic atmosphere of bygone grace and serenity. Through the holocaust of war, they have preserved a fine grandfather clock and cupboards of warm old wood. There are miniature roses growing in pots on the window sill and handmade lace curtains at the window. On the walls there are paintings, all originals, his father's, and some work of contemporary Leningrad artists. There is a large portrait of his mother when she was a young red-head. On the wall between the two windows there is a photograph of a handsome young man with intense dark eyes; this is his father at age 33, shortly before his death.

Paisley shawls cover the two beds, which are made into couches during the day. The table by one bed is covered by a warm confusion of books, papers, pencils, an old gramophone and some records.

On a small table near the windows there is always a spray of flowers, a branch of lilacs, some wild lupin or night violets, white and purple, which perfume the air only at night. For tea, this table is covered with a lace tablecloth. In the corner, in front of the old clock, there is a footstool and on it sits a brass tea kettle with a teapot on top which is constantly filled and re-filled with boiling water in the manner of old samovars.

Evdokia Petrovna is growing old now. A warm, loyal and devoted person, she does not understand all of her son's fiery ideas. Often, he is a trial for her. But in the patient manner of Russian women from time immemorial, she makes his few clothes, repairs his shoes, cooks his meals, scolds him, cares for him, and loves him. Last year, she lost the sight of one eye. When the doctors told her not to bend down, she simply said, "It is possible to spend one's life without bowing—but not without stooping."

Constantine's mother has been retired for several years and they live precariously. Still there always seems to be enough for one more. Friends come in and out at all hours of the day or night. Constantine's mother makes tea, and still more tea while they talk the days and nights away. Back and forth she travels to the kitchen, bringing different kinds of jams she has made herself, all kept in fat blue Russian jars, their wide mouths carefully covered with wax paper. Her cookies always seem to have been freshly baked, although no one has ever noticed her doing it. If friends stay through meal hours (and they always seem to), she discreetly disappears again and emerges from the kitchen with stacks of blini and cranberry-jam and sour cream, or one of a dozen fine Russian soups—*Botvinia*—made with fresh green beet tops, *okroshka* made with her homemade *kvass* and fresh little radishes and cucumbers, green *schee* with sorrel. And with it all a sturdy pile of good black bread and butter. There is always a pitcher of fresh cranberry juice which Constantine drinks incessantly. Fresh cranberries are kept as the old sailing men of Maine used to pre-serve them, in a tightly-sealed jar filled with water where they last a winter through. Eggs are kept in rock salt on the window sill.

Evdokia Petrovna listens patiently while her son and his friends recite. Constantine chain smokes the cheapest brand of Russian cigarettes, which he prefers. He paces up and down, and recites in a melodious tongue, relishing the words, stressing the sounds.

★   ★   ★

During all his years of picaresque wanderings he has read and developed his two overwhelming passions—Russian eighteenth-century culture and the Russian language. He is drawn by the elegance, the sense of proportion, the creativity of the eighteenth century.

"We in the twentieth century are closer to the thinking of the eighteenth century than to the thinking of the nineteenth century," he says. "Art continually moves from analysis to synthesis. The nineteenth century was a great period of synthesis in art, but art was not created then. I believe art was created in the eighteenth century—the roots of Russian poetry lie in the eighteenth century. It is easy to create once someone has shown the way—made the form, if you will. Lawrence Sterne created the form of the modern novel in the eighteenth century. He called his work "Sentimental Journey" but it is not sentimental at all, it is close to the thinking of the twentieth century. In the eighteenth century new forms were created everywhere. And we too, in the twentieth century are looking again at *how* a thing is done. We are analysing art, not synthesizing.

"I think every art is like a crystal, searching to become perfect in form, striving for immortality, trying to become fixed forever. But art must be eternally alive and cannot be fixed permanently. This would be perfection, death—and the end of art. Therefore just before the crystal is made, it is time to melt it and look again at the materials of the crystal, to break it and begin again. It is necessary for us to seek our own form, to destroy old structures in order to make them alive again. The early period of the twentieth century was a high period of breaking the crystal, of searching—in painting, in music, in poetry, and in literature."

Kuzminsky is drawn to the elegance of the eighteenth century because he feels it offers a hopeful pattern for modern man: "We all have in us dark and earthy forces without form—but there is also such a thing as elegance and this is what is lacking in our age. How can we find time for style? And yet there is such a thing as aestheticism, there has been and there will be, not just as a device, but as a philosophical entity, as a form of perception."

Kuzminsky has read deeply in both Russian and foreign literature. He reads continually in English to improve his knowledge of the language—everything from detective stories to classics. He has struggled by himself to read French and has tried to write English poetry with the help of an 1894 dictionary. ("If I could," he says, "I would write music and paint, only to make my soul deeper, to understand.") Among French writers, he prefers Flaubert, France and de Regnier. He loves the "sweet sounds" of the English poets, particularly Byron and Swinburne. He quotes Kipling at length, admiring his strong sounds. He considers Lawrence Sterne the greatest English writer. Apart from Sterne's *Tristram Shandy* and *Sentimental Journey*, he cites three books as most important in the development of his own personal philosophy: Gabriel d'Annunzio's *Extreme Enjoyment*, Marinetti's *The Futurist Marfaka*, and Leonard Franck's *Man's God*.

Kuzminsky has studied all the Russian writers and poets, and is particularly interested in the ideas of the Futurist movement or the twenties, notably Khlebnikov and Kruchenykh, because of their experiments with language. He says, "There have always been two trends in Russian poetry, which are summarized by verses of Pushkin:

We were born for inspiration
For sweet sounds and for praying
(That is, poetry for poetry's sake)
and
I shall long be loved by the people
Because I awakened their goodness with my lyre
And in my cruel country celebrated freedom
and appealed for mercy for the downtrodden.

Exegi Monumentum

"The poetry of the nineteenth century was not concerned with form but was primarily interested in 'celebrating freedom'", he explains. During that period, poetry was mostly applied to various political schemes and ideas. Fiet and Tiutchev were exceptions.

"In the early twentieth century there was a great interest in form. The Symbolists said, 'First clean the words, then take away any attributive sense from them.' They cleaned the language and disembodied it. The Acmeists, Gumiliev, Mandelstam and Zenkevich tried to give body to the word and the Futurists made the word Tsar. The Futurists were mostly laughed at and only young Mayakovsky was influenced by them. But then Mayakovsky with his "committed" poetry killed the poets of the thirties.

"Now it is our disease—the Russian language. The literary language that we lost in 1937. Only a very few people could carry the language proper and true during those terrible years. The poets taught by Akhmatova (Brodsky, Naiman, Rein) were able to take her language and her taste. This is a very strong group in Leningrad. Arseny Tarkovsky is now much in fashion, his poetry is a survival of this literary language. Today Akhmatova, Mandelstam, Pasternak, Mayakovsky and Tsvetayeva are very popular and strong influences on poets.

"But this survival of a literary language is not the same language we need for today. We need our own language. The émigré language is correct, but dead. Yevtushenko imitates Mayakovsky. Only Voznesensky has found his own voice—he has the eye of a painter and the ear of a poet. We must build foundations and we have few teachers."

On this question of the Russian language, Kuzminsky is fierce and intransigent. Russians generally are more tolerant than other people about hearing their own language imperfectly used, but not he. Kuzminsky regards it as a treasure not to be sullied or corrupted. He detests slang and the foreign words that are now prevalent, particularly among the young. In his pocket, he always carries a note-book with jottings for verses and in his neat careful handwriting, a study of Russian syllables counted as to frequency of use. With these word studies he is developing his own theories of sound in poetry:

"There are three kinds of poets—those who first hear and then see. Those who first see and then make a sound. And those who think in metaphors.

"I am the first kind; I believe in sound. My poetry is based mainly on sounds, the organizations of sounds, images made from sounds; although of course there must be sense as well. Our fathers in theory are the 1916 *Opoyaz*,* Brik, and his theoretical articles on poetry. Then back to the eighteenth century where the roots of Russian poetry lie. Brik talked about simple repetitions of sound—never synonyms, only homonyms. Sometimes it worked well, sometimes it was amusing. But it isn't music yet. It has only one drum and music must be polyphonical. We have a long way to go to learn polyphonic poetry."

Although he likes to experiment, Kuzminsky is strongly opposed to random and radical breaking of poetical disciplines. On the contrary, he warns, "Breaking the structure of verse is dangerous, especially for beginners. No discipline and too much freedom. One must first learn to construct and then you can do what you want. It is necessary to know *what* to destroy."

Kuzminsky has written a great deal. Some of his work is purely experimental. For this reason, he has been accused of being a "formalist". He is forever losing or giving away his work to friends or simply throwing it away because he feels it is not artistically successful. For the past four years he has been working on a massive poem called "The Tower of Babylon". Its form has

* Society for "The Study of Poetic Language (Obshchestvo po izucheniu poeticheskogo yazika).

often changed. It is an ambitious, complicated and highly experimental work. He has written many separate poems and poetic sections for this work, many thousands of lines, but he keeps throwing out pieces, rearranging them, creating new ones. The first poems make use of old Slavonic words. The poem then progresses in form and structure to completely modern language. Within this work there are also verses in French, English, Latin, and German.

In the section in this book, only the *Russian-Turkish Company*, and the small section called *Legend of Babylon* are from this work. The remaining poems are early efforts, a selection from his many love lyrics. Because of the complexity of the language and the reliance on sound images, his best work is impossible to translate. He understands and even desires this, because as he says, "Poetry is the concentrated beauty of a language. It is national and therefore in essence, untranslatable, because if it loses its own country, it loses everything. There can be poetry of language if you have an ear. Each sound has its own spirit, sound is emotional. It is helpful to hear the sounding of other languages. I believe that there will come a time in the future when poets will communicate not only with words, but with sounds."

A SPANISH CHAPTER

The arenas of Córdova red with bleeding
matadors, red the alleys. The sunset in the summer
of A.D. nineteen hundred and sixty-eight dies over Valencia.

The torero has no amulet,
only a muleta . . .
Clack of castanets. Cicádas
                        sultanas
                        pesetas
                        sunsettings
                                    sun
give way to piastered stars.
And in the shot-molten sky
crucified
matadors,
and night, a bull, over the body of Christ.

The day began with clatter of china.
A dawn broke scorching Córdova.
In the arena a torero.
In the stands, diaphanously modest, blushing gossamer.

And straining against the chaining cordon,
the crowd toss flowers—tosses smiles of women.
So, was the torero
feted by Córdova.

Horn of a bull to pummel
his vitals: cape in the sawdust, puddle
of blood . . . How shy you were
with the kisses you gave in the hotel chamber!

ГЛАВА ГИШПАНСКАЯ

На аренах Кордовы алеет кровь матадоров,
и алея, закат догорал над Валенсией в лето
тысяча девятьсот шестьдесят восьмое от Рождества

Христова.

А у тореро не было амулета.
Одна мулета.
Кастаньеты звенели, цикады
                    цукаты
                    закаты
                    дукаты
                                    солнца
сменялись на звезд пиастры.
Это на небе пестром —
распяты
матадоры
и ночь — быком — над телом Христовым.

День начинался стуком тарелок,
горела восходом зари Кордова.
На арене — тореро,
а в ложах стыдливо алела прозрачность капрона.

Силясь прорвать цепочку кордона,
толпа осыпала цветами, улыбками женщин парила —
так встречала Кордова
тореро.

В животе — рог быка —
и кровавая лужа плаща на опилках арены.
О как ты была робка,
в номерах мне объятья дарила.

It is the sunset
which ensanguines sand and sawdust,
bartering colour for blood.
Oh how ardently
you clasped me in embraces!

Night:
bull's ghost heavy on the city,
its carcass smothering sleepers.
You, your fingers to your throat:
you understood.

Stars,
rubbing on each other, clinking
incandescent with cold fire.
You, you fight for breath and stifle,
embracing a cadaver.

The morning will follow;
the dawn will rise on Córdova;
the sun will flood this earth incarnadine;
the ruddy phantom take to shadow.

There is no Córdova, Valencia—no such city.
No whetted horn to gash my mortal flesh;
and there will be no ghoul to follow.
So, call, call. I am ready.

And the world as an arena will unfold.

P.R.

Это закат
красным окрасил пыль и опилки,
краску на кровь обменяв.
О как пылко
ты в объятьях душила меня!

Ночь.
Это призрак быка навалился на город,
спящих тушей подмяв.
Это ты сжимаешь пальцами горло,
поняв.

Звезды.
Позвякивая, друг о друга трутся,
холодным горя огнём.
Это ты, в объятиях трупа,
задохнулась об нём.

Встанет утро,
заря над Кордовой воскреснет (махровая),
и багровое солнце зальет этот мир.
И кровавый призрак, прихрамывая,
удалится в объятья тьмы.

И нет Кордовы, Валенсии и прочих городов,
и рога нет, заточенного на плоть мою бренную,
и не будет призрака.
Позови. Я — готов.

И ляжет земля ареною.

A BEGGAR AND NAKED, I AM COLD

A beggar and naked, I am cold,
my one and only friend—the word.

The word rings, the word sings,
only the word comprehends

me. I will train myself to bow
down to your feet: the word as you.

Have all my blood at a single gulp!
. . . The word is a bell, the word rings.

The word rings, the word sings,
and the drone of the tombs overwhelms

me. Hunger approaches with rumbling pangs,
like a huge-headed chub the word floats up.

Under my teeth I crunch the word.
Alas! I remain hungry and cold.

P.R.

Я ХОЛОДЕН. Я НИЩ И ГОЛ

Я холоден. Я нищ и гол.
Мой друг единственный — глагол.

Глагол гудит, глагол поет,
глагол один меня поймет.

К тебе привыкну, как глагол,
к ногам приникну я главой.

Всю кровь мою — одним глотком!
...Как колокол, гудит глагол.

Глагол гудит, глагол поет,
и гул могил меня проймет.

И голод близится, как гул,
как голавль, плывет глагол.

На зуб попробовал глагол —
увы! — я голоден и гол.

THE RUSSIAN–TURKISH CAMPAIGN OF 1770

In the fantasy of Voltaire: Babylonian chariots swarming
as Count Rumyantsev dreams of the marshal's order adorning
his neck; and the unbelievers churned to the ground by the
   scything
spokes; and the prairies soaked with blood, spilt ordure piling;
holes ripped by enemy cannon—caverns yawning—
as the flood of the Oder is breached, armies of Prussians pouring
across . . . The hermit of Fernay sleeps on the bed of his pondering;
busts with blank eyes gaze at the island of Phores sung by
citharas and all those trampled shores of Hellas
where Agamemnon, King, is sepulchred with treasures
deep in his stony eyes and clouds like celestial lather
cover the wilderness—bloody
the word Peloponnesus—and the spare battalions of Spartans
where hands flung wide on the stones of Missolonghi: fastened
high on a stake hangs the blight from a lying nod
of Ypsilanti's head over the gates of ruined Troy
three heads from the single neck of Atreus sprouting
as Leander swims the Straits to a Schliemann waiting
and oleander petals scatter over Lygian
helmets. As the chariots of Solomon's biblical legions
go thundering by, Zuleika timidly presses
close to the breast of Suleiman, there where East–West rises
eclipsing the acropolis: the age-old
city of Oleg and Olga—my Constantinople—
whither the black waters race of the sea of Euxine
and resting from his exploits the Sublime
Porte on his sofa there reclines.

P. R.

РУССКО-ТУРЕЦКАЯ КАМПАНИЯ
1770-ОГО ГОДА

колесниц вавилонских вольтером измысленных орды
когда снится на шее румянцева графа фельдмаршальский

орден

когда спицы с серпами срезают под корень неверных
на равнинах исполненных крови и пролитой скверны
как каверны зияют следы неприятельских ядер
и войска пруссаков переходят разлившийся одер
на одре своих дум задремавший пустынник фернейский
смотрят бюсты глазами пустыми на остров форесский
кифаредом воспетый и стоптанный берег эллады
где зарыт агамемнон в глазах его каменных клады
словно пена небес облака над пустыней кровавы
слово пелопонесс и спартанцев сухие когорты
там где руки раскинув упал на камнях миссалонги
тот оболганный лживым кивком головы ипсиланти
на высоком колу у ворот развалившейся трои
эти трое голов отсеченных от шеи атрея
и проливом леандр проплывает там ждет его шлиман
и роняет цветы олеандр осыпая лигийские шлемы
и летят колесницы библейских полков соломона
и несмело прижмётся зюлейка к груди сулеймана
там где запад восток восстает затмевая акрополь
древний город олега и ольги мой константинополь
и стремятся к нему черны воды евксинского понта
и лежит на тахте отдыхая от подвигов порта

A CHAPTER ABOUT CROSSES

A cross. Did King Xerxes know?
Cross-crowned, a firm fortress stood.
A finger in Christ's deep wound,
at the cross of men's always-faith.
A finger—now and for all time—
a finger is pointed down.
The Persian, to mount his throne,
had vaulted upon the cross.
A temple hangs upside down;
the walls of it laugh and squeal.
Beneath a high crown of wounds
the cross's sharp slope spells fear.
A cross. Did King Xerxes know?
The top of these hills is grey.
I've ceased to complain, for strong
as that finger is man's crossed faith.
Is believing in you a cross?
A dirty and crusted sin.
The river of Zion's stars:
"And now—o my Son—a Greek."
Did Gracchus believe in God?
The enemy's crafty, strong.
The wounds of our onion tears
are a stone in the enemy's hand.
It sinks, and the blue of stars
cannot cover the roar of wounds
on the cross's high sounding-board.
"My Son is no more." He is.
That cross had been shaped of bronze—
Long ago—in these lofty hills.
Let them sing, let them loudly sing,
with the bronze of their muted throats.

КРЕСТОВАЯ ГЛАВА

Крест. Знал ли Ксеркс — крест?
Крепость — крестом вверх.
В рану Христа — перст
присно крестом вер.
Ныне и присно — перст.
Просто — перстом — вниз.
Принял престол перс
и на кресте вис.
Вниз головой — храм,
хохот и визг стен.
И под венцом ран
страшен креста крен.
Крест. Знал ли Ксеркс — крест?
Сер этих гор верх.
Я не ропщу — перст
присно крестом вер.
Вера в тебя — крест?
Грязной коростой грех.
Рек на Сионе звезд:
«Сыне — и ныне — грек.»
Верил ли Гракх — в рай?
Враг силен и лукав.
Луковых слез — ран
в руку врага (камень)
Канет рука. Днесь
синь этих звезд звон
ран на кресте — несть
«Сыне — не бысть!» — Он.
Оное время — медь.
Крест. — Посреди гор.
Да посвятят петь
медью немых горл!

For now I shall pray—a cross.
That Persian was still no Greek.★
And fearful is now the finger
of fate among the stars.

G.L.K.

★ Literally, "The Persian who has not become a Greek," presumably a reference to Xerxes, who would have "become a Greek" if he had succeeded in conquering the Greek city-states during the Persian Wars.

Ныне молюсь — крест. —
Греком не ставший перс. —
И посреди звезд
страшен судьбы перст.

FOG •

So silver, in the city,
                    fog.
Settling down on the head,
                              fog.
Solitary and cold,
                    fog.
Clasp her closely,
                    fog.
Search her eyes deeply,
                          fog.
Fall on her shoulders,
                        fog.
Embrace her, as I once embraced her.
. . . . Not forgetting her shoulder,
                                  fog.
The houses are frozen in fog.
So deceive,
              and beckon,
                            fog.
Stillness,
          and pale gloom.
Neither you . . .
                    nor me.
Fog. . .

ТУМАН

И.Х.

Очень серый
                    в городе туман.
Облепляет голову
                    туман.
Одинок и холоден
                    туман.
Серый
        в сером городе
                    туман.
Обними её крепче,
                    туман.
Загляни ей в глаза,
                    туман.
Упади ей на плечи,
                    туман.
Обними,
        как меия обнимал.
...Не забыть Её плеч,
                    туман,
не забыть Её плач —
                    обман.
Замерзают в тумане
                    дома.
То обманет,
        то манит
                    туман.
Тишина
        и белёсая тьма.
Ни тебя...
            Ни меня.
Туман...

JAM SESSION

Me and Jones are hep
on the well-turned hip
we finger the line of the belly

We grunt and we flip
We jig tru-la-la

Me and Jones
Jonathan Jones

The fiddle sings
with its—oh—split lip
The oboe is yelling

about her undressed
midriff and yes
we trample and burst
with a "wow!" from within
and bubbles without

Sing
Jonathan Jones
of her midriff unclad

Sing
of her eyes
so dark and so sad
where the lamp-posts stand
and don't give a damn
Sing
of her breasts
with their dawn suppleness

No, just you watch
the drummer drum his shocks

Sing
Jonathan Jones

P.R.

ДЖАЗОВЫЙ ПРОИГРЫШ

Я и Джонс — мастера
тонкого бедра
мы трогаем линию на животе

хрюкнем, ногнем
спляшем тру-ля-ля

Я и Джонс,
Джонатан Джонс

Скрипка поет
О как рассеченной губой
воет гобой

о ее
бедрах обнаженных

топнем, лопнем
как пузыри
бедра снаружи
а вопль внутри

Пой,
Джонатан Джонс
о ее
бедрах обнаженных

пой
о зрачках
темных и печальных
там, где фонари
дергают плечами

пой
о ее груди
упругой утрами

нет, ты только погляди
как прыгает ударник

пой,
Джонатан Джонс

WHEN YOU LEAVE THE FLOWERS STAY

When you leave, the flowers stay
and my fixed constancy, with rhymes distilled
  from this most timid prayer—stay!
  (O verses wrung out from these moments' longing!)
When you depart, desert, and fly away,
  how terrible it is!
  For you were here embracing, giving, brimming
  with those full bows, your lips. O stay!
When you depart and when the cosmos shrinks
  to a window-chink, a man condemned for life will say:
  Judge me not for my rash judgments, wait . . .
  (No, I must wait—for you—and keep from fitful hopes
  and fears; fulfilled, fulfillable) . . . O where are you?
  Habiliments that you left off breathe hope, delight—
  I crush you in my arms.
When you depart, the walls ring cold with laughter and my
      moans
  are barely heard. Ah, is this distance not
  too far from him abandoned to be hurt.
  It is my yearning, not remorse, that fetters me:
  my world is split, the coldness of these stones
  leans closer on me, and the sweating walls grow inwards, slow:
  the space between, a slit
  of terror—O my lodestone, you! . . . But I,
When you depart—I stay, flattened, crucified
  against the wall (no, do not ask what happens
  if I stay), your lips grow frigid
  though I branded them with kisses.
But when I stay, it is with all that damaged pride
  and bitter diffidence you handed
  me: imploring, pleading, calling out your name,
  misunderstood by all and torn away
  into the ether, helpless, useless . . . O my cry!
  O name breathed out with such a sigh!

КОГДА ТЫ УЕЗЖАЕШЬ, ОСТАЮТСЯ ЦВЕТЫ

Когда ты уезжаешь, остаются цветы.
Остается мое постоянство и стихи, настоенные на стыдливой
    мольбе — останься!
    О, стансы, написанные в минуты тоски по тебе!
Когда ты уезжаешь, улетаешь, уходишь — ах, как это
    нехорошо;
    когда ты оставалась, обнимала, отдавала округлые
                                губы
    свои — о, останься!
Но когда ты уезжаешь, когда сужается мир, как окно перед
    осужденным на пожизненное заключение — не
                         осуждай меня
    за мои опрометчивые суждения, — жди и
    нет, это я должен ждать тебя, сдерживаясь от
                      судорожных
    надежд и ужасов — уже свершившегося и
                        ожидающего
    завершения — о где ж ты!
    Сброшенные одежды, надежду сулящие, вселяющие
                      веселие
    в душу — в объятьях душу тебя
но когда ты уходишь, холодным хохотом отзываются стены —
    стенания мои не слышны: не слишком ли велико
                      расстояние,
    растерзанию предоставленного
    не раскаяние сковывает руки мои — тоской по
                  тебе, когда
    мир расколот — холод камней ко мне склоненных —
    ослизлых стен постепенное (пространства меж ними)
    суживание
    с ужасом — Суженая моя! Но я
когда ты уходишь, остаюсь, тобою распластанный (распятый
    на стене — о нет!) — не расспрашивай, если я
                  остаюсь —
    и уста остывают твои от моих поцелуев горячечных,

When you depart,
   no when you are in my ears,
   be a voice that speaks, say fiery things
   against my too brash words, but also hear
   the songs I sang for you, and see the fluttering eye
   that looks at you in awe, that shrinks last joys
   into calls and cries and yells and yelping
   pangs from him who whining, anguished, ravished, cold,
   hurt and pleading chants:
   O no! Which spells
When you depart

P.R.

когда я остаюсь. Гордостью и робостью руки (руки твоей)
вымаливающий, вымалчивающий имя твое, ими не
понятое —
поднятое до небес беспомощным (бесполезным)
криком моим
о имя выдохом высказанное
когда ты ушла
нет, когда ты в ушах — голосом, говором, выговором
негодования твоего на мои неугодные речи —
речитативом
пропетые песни тебе, плеском зрачков на тебя
удивленно
взирающих, вбирающих радость последнюю,
взывающих,
плачущих, воющих, кричащих от боли, тоскою
скулящих,
голодных, хладных, ноющих и молящих, поющих
(о нет!),
визжащих

когда уезжаешь ты

TALE OF BABYLON

There was a city, Babylon,
where flowers no longer grew,
this city did not rule the world:
the world was ruled by You.

There, on a bend in the river,
where an island beetled high,
with a wave of your hand a tower's
foundations rose to the sky.

The Tower was waxing wider,
mortar mixed by hands.
To finish it they needed
another month in hand.

All laboured on the Tower:
the maimed, the old, the young;
or else unto the seventh
generation all were hung.

Higher they heaped the boulders,
shirts bloodied in sweat.
The unforgivable sin was
to hold the Tower in doubt.

Stone upon stone was heaped there,
Stones heaved higher than heaven.
And turbid silent teardrops
rolled down in a ribbon.

Curdled blood and gore then
dripped down from above.
You reigned over the Tower:
the Tower's name was Love.

ПОВЕСТЬ О ВАВИЛОНЕ

Город был Вавилон,
в нем не росли цветы,
миром не правил он,
миром правила Ты.

Там, на изгиб реки,
где возвышался остров,
взмахом Твоей руки
башни взметнулся остов.

Башня росла вширь,
руки раствор месят,
чтобы ее завершить,
требовался месяц.

Башню строили все —
стар, и млад, и калека.
За отказ — всем им висеть
вплоть до седьмого колена.

Камни катили вверх,
кровью потели рубашки.
Самый большой Грех
был — сомнение в Башне.

Камень на камень лез,
камень над небом вис.
Мутные реки слез
молча катились вниз.

Свертывалась кровь,
капая с высоты.
Башня звалась Любовь,
Башней правила Ты.

Stone crawled upon stonework,
Stone was poised on stone.
And hate pressed on the Tower
dark red welts of roan.

. . . The city, O, was Babylon,
and there no flowers grew:
famous just its Tower,
but on the Tower sat You.

Love is dead: waft incense,
Our common language gone.
We sit like infants trying
Love's ABC's to con.

And trying to grasp the rapture
of kisses, touch of hands,
chant imperious ALLELUIA!
so others understand.

Over dead love a cerecloth
of clouds and waters merge,
and corpses cold of beauties
obscenely lead a dirge.

Over dead love a stillness,
flutter of wings and chitter.
Yet in the night I wake: my
groping arms search you.

P.R.

И камень на камень полз,
и камень на камне вис.
И темно-красные полосы
на Башне оставила ненависть.

...Город был Вавилон,
в нем не росли цветы.
Лишь Башней славился он,
на Башне сидела Ты.

Над умершей Любовью кадите:
потеряли мы общий язык,
и сидим с букварями, как дети,
и любви постигаем азы.

Постигаем восторг поцелуя,
предвкушаем пожатье руки,
велегласно поем «Аллилуйя!»,
заодно обучая других.

Над умершей Любовью, как саван,
облака — продолжением вод,
и холодные трупы красавиц
нехороший ведут хоровод.

Над умершей Любовью — молчанье,
крыл мелькание и щебетня...

Только я просыпаюсь ночами,
и рука моя ищет тебя.

Interpret who pursues me,
dragomen slanted-of-eye.
The Tartar horsemen slyly
stalked Russia in the night.

The green breasts of the clearings
have garnered guiltless blood.
Captives rapt, on lathering
horses' saddles flung.

The echo of their raging
hoof-beat thunder fades.
To the sun-ringing steppe they
dragged their captive prey.

Bitter the dust-white grasslands,
under the boundless sky
they laid them, all alone, there,
and from them children surged.

I shall forever champion
the trampled rights of love:
the slit-eyed Mamay spoiled the
Russianess in Russian blood

And this trace ages later
alone of them has strayed
the strange eyes of the gazer
chase us down each age.

P.R.

ОТСТУПЛЕНИЕ О ФОРМЕ ГЛАЗ

Растолкуйте мне, кто за мной гонится,
скуластые толмачи.
Наметом татарская конница
на Русь пробиралась в ночи.

Зеленые груди полянок
невинную кровь хранят.
Бросали они полонянок
на взмыленный круп коня.

И топот копыт, обидчив,
глухим бормотаньем стих.
Влачили они добычу
в звенящую солнцем степь.

В полыни, белой от пыли,
под небом бездонным одни,
они полонянок любили,
и дети пошли от них.

Буду навек поборником —
попранных прав любви:
косым Мамаем попорчена
русость в русской крови.

Века прошли. Эта веха
от них осталась одна.
И странная форма века
веками преследует нас.

YOU ARE MY EARTH

You are my Earth: I—Antéus.
Try now to tear me away or untie us.
My poem and I are chained to dying,
yet all my words about her are quiet.

You are my poem and downward ruin.
You are the flight of my trembling wings.
But the wax on those wings has melted away
from the beat of our sun and heady day.

I fall to the ground: Icarus. I
roamed like a ghost in search of you.
Fortunate Providence brought us together
in order to make me glitter with words.

I tumble on you, Earth, my Gaea.
The mountains, villages, how familiar!
The final news, the last bulletin
—bitter—will be that you are mine.

P.R.

ТЫ — ЗЕМЛЯ МОЯ. А Я — АНТЕЙ

Ты — Земля моя. А я — Антей.
Оторви теперь меня, попробуй!
Мы поэмой скованы до гроба,
все слова мои молчат — о ней.

Ты моя поэма и паденье,
ты — паренье трепетных воскрылий,
только воск, растаявший на крыльях,
наше Солнце — наше наслажденье.

Я ударюсь оземь. Я — Икар.
Я тебя искал, как привиденье.
Нас свело благое Провиденье,
чтобы я словьями засверкал.

О тебя ударюсь. Ты — Земля.
Как знакомы горы все и веси!
И последним горестным известьем
будет то, что будешь ты моя.

THE SEASON IS AUTUMN

The season is autumn. In the pitch-blue sky
rent clouds. Rain in Alupka. Night.
In a deserted shack I drink pertsovka. My
reason tells me that my brain
is idle and that I
am garbled, nameless. I am mute . . .
Torrents flush the dirty streets:
the cornices like cascades; the cypresses
like phantoms, standing. Houses in retreat
towards the shadows. Tears streak
the whitewash . . . The caprice
of southern climes is past belief.
So do our heirs ungratefully
poke their fingers at the sky.
My God! On the banks of the Tauris, they
may not drink; and crystalline
are the Cyprides of fantasy . . .
and so, within the rhythm
of verses, suffering is contained.
God! The sobs proliferate,
the chasms grow
wider, and the booby moon
slides in a melanic sky,
rolling in and out of clouds. The cry
for bread and for the crumbling blue
of skies. My ghost is restless. Oh, with us
nothing will materialize.
. . . But the cross remains on our shoulders—
insomnia, Golgotha, dreams.

P.R.—S.M.

342

Сезон осенний. В небе сизом
разрывы туч. Дожди в Алупке.
И ночь. В заброшенной халупке
я пью перцовую. Мой разум
мне говорит, что мозг мой празден,
что я не понят и не признан.
И я молчу. И мчат потоки
по грязным улицам. Карнизы —
как водопады. Кипарисы
стоят как призраки. В потемки
дома уходят. Слез потоки
на белой извести. Капризы
погоды южной не представишь.
Как в небо тыкают перстами
неблагодарные потомки,
мой Бог! На берегах Тавриды
им не пристало пить. Кристальны
Киприды выдумки. Так в ритм
стихов — уложатся страданья.
О Боже, множатся рыданья:
разверсты хляби. В чёрном небе
луны безумное круженье
меж туч. Моление о хлебе
и голубых небес крушенье.
Мой призрак беспокойный с нами
ничто не должно приключиться.
...Но крест пребудет при ключицах —
бессонницей, Голгофой, снами.

BIBLIOGRAPHICAL NOTE

The editor consulted and drew material from the following Soviet publications: *Triptykh* by Victor Sosnora, Lenizdat 1965; *Vsadniki* by Victor Sosnora, Lenizdat 1969; *Kosiya Suchiya* by Gleb Gorbovsky, Sovetsky Pisatel, Leningrad 1966; *Tishina* by Gleb Gorbovsky, Lenizdat 1967; *Novoye Leto* by Gleb Gorbovsky, Sovetsky Pisatel, Leningrad 1970; *Nochnoy Dozor* by Alexander Kushner, Sovetsky Pisatel, Leningrad 1966; *Primety* by Alexander Kushner, Leningrad 1969; also from *Den Poezii*, Sovetsky Pisatel, Leningrad 1967, 1968, 1969; *Molodoy Leningrad*, Sovetsky Pisatel, Leningrad 1968; *Zvezda*, Khudozhestvennaya Literatura, Leningrad, 1968. The poems of Joseph Brodsky were taken from *Ostanovka v pustyne*, Chekhov Press, New York 1970. Among the general works consulted, particularly useful were: *Modern Russian Poetry* ed. V. Markov and M. Sparks, Bobbs Merrill and Macgibbon and Kee 1967; *Russian Futurism:* University of California Press 1968; *The 900 Days* by Harrison Salisbury, Harper and Row, 1969; *The Icon and the Axe* by James Billington, Alfred Knopf 1966; *Gorod Velikogo Lenina*, Lenizdat 1957.